With love & Joy

from Ashley Silver

She Came To Heal

abbey silva

authorHOUSE®

Please post your
comments on
www.shecametoheal.com

AuthorHouse™
1663 Liberty Drive, Suite 200
Bloomington, IN 47403
www.authorhouse.com
Phone: 1-800-839-8640

This book is a work of non-fiction. Unless otherwise noted, the author and the publisher make no explicit guarantees as to the accuracy of the information contained in this book and in some cases, names of people and places have been altered to protect their privacy.

First published by AuthorHouse   11/26/2008

ISBN: 978-1-4389-1086-4 (sc)

Printed in the United States of America
Bloomington, Indiana

This book is printed on acid-free paper.

This book is dedicated to all the parents and families of a Down Syndrome child. To Joy Elizabeth's two brothers, her father, and her loving family and friends.

Special Thanks

Book Cover designed by John Kerr around a photo of a beautiful

Cattelaya Washburn Orchid that bloomed on

October 27, 2007 in the orchid room at their residence in

Twin Falls, Idaho.

The orchid was purchased at the Magic Valley Orchid

Society show on October 14, 2007,

Twin Falls, Idaho

"We are honored, to design this cover. Because of Joy Elizabeth,
We met and married."

John and Marion Kerr

Prologue

This is a true story. It is a story about loving, longing, heartache and healing. It is a story about contracts – ones that we make with others before coming into this experience called living. It is the story of Annie's tenacity to find healing for her baby daughter. It's the unfolding of events in her search for that wholeness. It's the saga of those moments, days, months and years in Annie's on going goal to find healing for her child, her twenty-four hour crib baby, diagnosed with Down's Syndrome. It's all about baby Joy Elizabeth.

It is the story of Joy's contract with her mother, her father, her two half-brothers and many others as well, who came into her space.

It is a story that has been aching to be told for over forty years. It touches on the many aspects operating in Annie's life at the time; each one being played out on the screen called living "Now." It is Annie's wish in telling this story even more healing will come to those whose paths have crossed Joy Elizabeth's. It is the gratitude for Joy in Annie's heart for the healing received, for the spiritual growth that followed, that births the sharing of this story at this time.

It will become very obvious to the reader that "JOY IS AN INSIDE JOB THAT HEALS." The reader will become very aware of how God answers prayer. You will become acutely aware of how the answers don't always come the way you want them to. Neither does it happen the way you intended, but it happens. It happens in ways you would never dream of, but the way it happens is the way it was meant to happen. It happens, it happened, and Joy Elizabeth fulfilled her mission. Now it is time to tell her story.

The names of everyone except Joy Elizabeth are fictitious. This is in order to protect the privacy of those who may still find the pain too difficult to deal with, and may not wish to be reminded of their part in her life. Her story is meant to be told.

The life of Joy Elizabeth begins on Memorial Day, 1966. Interestingly, this is a day of remembering. Remembering what? Remembering, those who died serving our country. Remembering, those we made contracts with before coming into this experience. Remembering, the choices we made about our experiences. Remembering, previous lifetimes and the parts we played in them. Remembering, how God works, when we let go and let God. Remembering, in the end, we are all one.

Joy Elizabeth's mother, Annie, tells the story. She is grateful that Baby Joy came into her life. She is grateful for the insight she received caring for her daughter Joy. She will be ever grateful for the healing that Joy Elizabeth brought into her life. She is grateful for the God of love she found, for the God she loved, often doubted and sometimes trusted. The God she regularly argued with, sometimes praised, and was often angry with. This is the God Annie railed at on more than one occasion. Annie learned to let God unfold life in his perfect way. Like the prodigal son, Annie too wandered far from love, but in the end returned home to all that she was. Joy Elizabeth, Annie's daughter truly was an orchid.

Table of Contents

1

BEFORE JOY

Annie had been divorced from her sons' father for over two years now, separated even longer. She was working as a waitress at a country club. At the present time she lived in one of the family homes they had built together before they divorced. They had two sons, Bryan, who was fourteen and Paul, who was eleven. Annie had moved back to the bay area from San Diego. She was running from a relationship gone bad to make a new start in life. Annie wanted to make it easier for her sons to spend more time with their father. They both loved the boys, and both of the boys needed the presence of both their parents.

Annie had begun to make new friends and participate in activities at church. She was taking swimming lessons at the local gym to overcome a fear of drowning. She had joined a local singles group that met in various homes. Annie had gone on several outings with the group. Most everyone in the group were single parents, some alone, some with their children, and all needing friends.

One day Annie met Jeff, a high school teacher and coach from a neighboring town, and they hit it off quite well. They had rapport with each other almost from the beginning. They talked of many things, life, philosophy, beliefs, education and their children. Jeff was great with Annie's sons, often stopping by after his coaching duties to toss a football back and forth with Bryan and Paul. He and Bryan talked at length about history, which was Jeff's minor in college. They often discussed how it affected the present. History was not a favorite subject of Bryan's, who often complained that he could see no reason for studying it. Jeff agreed with Bryan on the importance of current events which were applicable. He emphasized to Bryan that the study of history would greatly enhance Bryan's understanding of what those current events meant. He explained to Bryan how history repeats itself.

Jeff was comfortable with the boys, and they were with him. Jeff always made time for them. Annie and Jeff were together often during the summer and fall of 1965. They shared an uncanny sense of ESP between them, a new experience for both of them.

One day the boys had expressed a desire for Annie to make a German Chocolate cake for dinner. Annie had to work, thought about it while she worked and decided to make the cake. Jeff arrived while Annie was unloading her car. He had bought and brought with him a German

Chocolate cake. Jeff told Bryan and Paul at dinner he was driving through town when something said go in and buy a cake, a German Chocolate cake. He told them how he parked his convertible, jumped out and ran into the best bakery in town. Over dinner when Jeff heard they had asked for the cake, he said he got their message. Jeff made being alive fun and interesting.. He was that kind of person.

Then Annie discovered she was pregnant. All those years of wanting to have a baby daughter, it had not happened while she was married to her sons' father. After all those years longing for a daughter, Annie had mixed feelings. Annie was not happy that she was pregnant and unmarried. Jeff was not happy about it either. Annie and Jeff agreed to keep their relationship at a low profile due to his teaching position.

Annie continued to work until late in February. Then morning sickness and being on her feet for long periods became unbearable. Jeff was making himself less available to Annie. She had a strong feeling he was going to split and not be there, for either of them, when the time came.

Before Annie had moved back to the bay area, she had discovered a God of love while living in San Diego. This had happened shortly after her separation from the boys' father. At that time she chose to pack up the boys, the household and move away from where the pain of the marriage break-up had become so unbearable. Annie was finding this God of love in the Unity Church. She and the boys were attending services with the boys' grandmother. This God of love was totally opposite of what she experienced growing up. Annie had only known a God she was afraid of, a God who spoke of damnation, hell fire and brimstone. Annie had grown up with a dreadful fear of God. The God she had grown up with would get you even if you did watch out.

Suddenly, this God of love was beginning to be Annie's only solace. She read everything she could find about this God of love, about joyous living, and about forgiveness. This new concept was wrapping Annie up in its ideas on a daily basis. Annie prayed constantly for insight, and help. She wanted to experience this love she had been learning about.

It was Annie's only salvation during the months of pregnancy. She was learning about taking responsibility for where she was in life. She was learning what choice was about. Annie began to change her thoughts and attitudes from resentment and anger to forgiveness and understanding. Annie was discovering what being at choice in her intentions was about and what she wanted to experience. Annie was so thankful that she had this God of love in her life.

2

BABY JOY IS BORN

It was Memorial Day, 1966 when baby decided it was time to be born. It was 1:05 a.m. and Annie was already at the hospital. This baby knew she would be accepted in this family. She knew she would be loved. She had made this contract a long time ago with both Annie and Jeff. The time was now; time for her to complete the mission she had come to fulfill. It made it so much easier knowing she would be loved. She knew, too, she had two half-brothers, Bryan and Paul, at home. She had known for sometime that her mother, Annie, had wanted a little girl, a daughter of her own. She was coming with problems. These problems would change the life of not only her mother, her father, her two half-brothers, but many others as well. This is the story of Joy Elizabeth, the story of her mother, Annie, the story of her two brothers, and the story of her father, Jeff, who chose to disappear.

Baby Joy Elizabeth weighed in at six pounds, nine ounces, twenty one inches long. She was diagnosed at birth with moderate Down Syndrome. She had physical problems as well: an inverted rib cage, a weak heart, and jaundice. But she was here! (Down Syndrome refers to common genetic disorders that result in birth defects, medical problems, and a degree of mental retardation.)

Baby Joy was whisked away to an incubator before Annie was able to hold her. The doctor informed her she had a baby girl. Annie heard her cry and then a nurse quickly removed her from the delivery room. Annie was happy that she had a baby girl, and suddenly was very tired.

The baby's father, Jeff, had come to the hospital sometime between her birth and morning. He had heard the doctor's diagnosis, seen his baby daughter, Joy. He signed her birth certificate, paid the hospital bill and left. After he left the hospital he told Maria, Annie's closest friend, that he could not face Annie, and he split.

The family friend, Keith, who had been instrumental in introducing Annie and Jeff, shared with her later about Jeff. Jeff had not only walked out on them, but also his teaching job two weeks before school was out. Jeff hadn't drawn a sober breath for six months according to their mutual friend, Keith. Annie knew he must be hurting badly because Jeff was not a drinker. Annie didn't really know what she felt for Jeff. She did feel abandoned, resentful, and angry that he chose to split.

She recognized a pattern in Jeff that she had observed in herself in the past. Jeff was still operating from a choice he had made early on to run when things went bad. He was not happy about the baby in the first place. Jeff was not aware of the contract he had made with Baby Joy, but Annie was.

Annie knew of her choice in the past to run and hide when she was in pain. Since she was a child, Annie had been running and hiding when things turned ugly. This was a decision she had made to survive, early in life. It had saved her many times as a child. Later on as an adult she packed up the boys and ran off during the bad times in her marriage.

But Annie had made a new decision about responsibility while she was pregnant with Joy. She accepted she was a pregnant unwed mother with two sons, one fourteen and one eleven. Annie was divorced from their father and on her own. She had decided six months into this pregnancy that she would never, ever, run from any situation, any problem, or anyone, ever again. That was a big decision for Annie. No matter what happened, how it happened, or who it happened to, she would stay and face the consequences. She realized it was up to her to choose again to run or stay.

Annie had learned that when we run from a problem, or deny it exists, or hide from it in any way, it always repeats itself down the path of life. She no longer wanted to repeat this experience, only to people it with new characters. Annie didn't want to experience the same plot. Each time the drama unfolded it became more intense. Annie wanted to take care of it where it was, right here, right now, and not run again. She was through with running. She had run for the last time.

After the baby was cleaned up and placed in the incubator, Annie was taken to her own room. Annie remembered how thankful she was to have the baby girl she wanted. She promised herself she would love this baby, care for her and let her know how much she was loved. Annie was tired; and fell into an exhausted sleep.

The next morning the doctor came after Annie had asked the nurses repeatedly to bring her baby daughter to her. Annie could hear the doctor in the hallway talking to the boys' father, and she was confused. She could not figure out why her ex-husband was at the hospital, and not Jeff, the baby's father. Had something happened to Jeff on his way back from the conference last night? Marie had promised Annie she would call him. Had something happened to one of the boys? They had gone to stay with their father and his new wife for the weekend.

Where was her baby daughter? The doctor finally came in. But still they had not brought Annie her baby. The doctor sat down beside Annie's bed. He looked tired and anxious. Annie sensed that he was the bearer of bad news.

The doctor finally shared with Annie that her daughter had Down's Syndrome, with physical problems as well. He said, "Your baby's retardation is more than moderate and most likely she will not live out the year." The doctor suggested Annie make arrangements to place the baby in Sonoma State Hospital to be cared for. The doctor went on to explain that keeping her at home would be a twenty-four hour job.

Annie had already decided she was going to take her home. She decided she would find a way to deal with her problems. She reasoned that sending this little new-born baby to someone or some place else to be cared for was another way of running. Annie was going to have no part of that. She would find the way to heal her baby daughter.

The baby, wrapped snuggly in blankets, was finally brought to Annie by the nurse. Annie looked at her daughter, and began undoing the blankets around the baby. She noted she had ten fingers, ten toes, two eyes, two ears, and little skinny legs and arms. Annie saw the swish of reddish brown hair about two inches long and ran her hands gently through it. Yes, she noticed the baby's face was flat, her eyes shaped like almonds, and she could see her rib cage was inverted as the doctor had said. Annie's daughter was beautiful. She recalled she felt the same way at the birth of both of her sons.

She made the decision to take her baby home. Somehow, she decided she would find a way to care for both the baby and her brothers. God would show her a way to heal her as well. She was certain one day she would prove the doctor wrong. Annie felt that one day her baby

would crawl, walk, run and play as her brothers had before her.

3

IT'S IN THE NAME

Annie chose the name for her baby well. "Joy", the very name Baby Joy had picked out to be called. Joy had also chosen to come on Memorial Day as well. She knew that in remembering her, Annie would recognize one day her mission this lifetime. Baby Joy knew it appeared her mother took the name from a book entitled, **"JOY IS AN INSIDE JOB."** The title tells it all. The author of the book was the former Poet Laureate of Hawaii, Don Blanding. The book is about Don Blanding's spiritual awakening. How apropos the title of this book was. Could there have been a divine plan here? Joy knew the name was perfect for the mission she had come to complete. The book had been a gift to Annie from her mother. Annie's mother was instrumental in Annie finding a God of love over three years ago, after years of only knowing a God of fear.

Annie picked the name "Elizabeth" from the Bible, which she had been reading with the Unity Interpretative Dictionary. Elizabeth was the name of John the Baptist's Mother. John was the harbinger, or messenger, to the people of his time. He called on them to prepare the way for the son of God to come into their lives. That son of God, Jesus, who taught and practiced unconditional love, who healed the sick, forgave sinners, and fed those who hungered. Elizabeth was past the child bearing age when she conceived John. Annie was in her late thirties and getting close to that age herself. Both names were perfect. Joy Elizabeth loved the names. How much better could it be? Joy Elizabeth knew she would be loved. That was what seemed so important at this time.

4

HOME IN TIME TO MOVE

Annie took Baby Joy home to a little three bedroom house on one of the town's main drags. Joy's two brothers, Bryan and Paul, lived there also but were still at their father's for another day or two. Annie had rented this small tract home because the rent was really reasonable. The home had been up for sale for over two years. She would have to move before the winter. The current owner had decided to take it off the market and move back in himself.

The boys' father was glad to know they planned to move before winter and hopefully before school started. This house was in an area known as the flood plane and more than once been flooded during the heavy rains in January and February. This was almost a sure thing if heavy rains persisted for more than three or four days, along with the high tides that affected run off in the area.

The river was often over its banks in the winter time. It made this an unsafe place for the boys, their mother and of course the new baby.

So at the beginning of September they moved to an older home in an older, more settled part of town. It was a long way from the flood plane area. It was a roomy older house with high ceilings, and a built in china cabinet/buffet separating the kitchen from the dining room. The hardwood floors were waxed to a luster. Grandma Gertrude helped put up curtains on the tall windows. The only drawback to the house was the garage, too old and too narrow for Annie's car, so the car had to sit out in the weather.

Here in the older house Joy was ensconced in her bassinet in the center of the living room. She could be watched closely here. She would be close to the heat, a large floor furnace between the living and dining room. Here she could be part of the activity with her brothers and her mother. Here Baby Joy was fed, diapered, sung to, rocked to sleep and prayed for on a daily basis. Here Annie looked with a keen eye, and a heart filled with desire, for every morsel of healing that could be found. Sun shining through the tall windows warmed the room, and filled the space with light.

Here each day as her brothers returned from school they would hunker over her bassinet and talk to Baby Joy. They would caress her cheeks, and sometimes sing to her. Both brothers had been told about Joy's physical problems. Annie was not sure either of them understood the degree of Baby Joy's problems. Even Annie was in denial of the full scope of what was termed more than moderate Down Syndrome.

5

FOUR MONTH PROGRESS REPORT

Annie knew Joy was not progressing according to the baby books Annie had for the boys. Baby Joy was going to be a slow baby. Baby Joy did not show much recognition; she rarely cried, and she continued to have difficulty breathing and feeding. She was still being fed every four hours, night and day, and only taking one and a half to two ounces of milk per feeding. Baby Joy rarely even tried to move her arms or legs, let alone her head. She could not lift her head at all when she lay on her tummy. She was having difficulty swallowing and her muscle structure was very weak. She was showing signs of being spastic as well as retarded. She had not smiled. She had a distant look in her eyes as if she were seeing something else. She seemed to be looking beyond Annie when her eyes were open.

She had not progressed to the growth of her two brothers at the same age, yet Annie did not give up hope that things would turn around. She so wanted little Joy to be able to live life fully and enjoy each day of it, and Annie was determined she would find the way.

There was not much help for parents of Down Syndrome children at this time, and even information seemed to be difficult and sparse when she could find it at all. She searched for anything she could find on the care and prognoses of Down Syndrome children.

Annie was not able to return to work because too much time was needed just to take care of Baby Joy. She continued to look for a way to bring in an income that would allow her to spend the necessary time with her baby, and her sons. Baby Joy was way too young to leave with her brothers while she worked. She began a search for organizations that could help her not only with Joy's care, but with other information that would be useful. Bryan was attending high school about five blocks away, and was a big help in watching Joy when Annie had to go for interviews for work, or to run errands, pay bills, and grocery shop. Paul was in junior high school and had farther to go to school, but could always be counted on for the chores that needed to be done at home. Both of Baby Joy's brothers were very responsible, attentive, and caring.

6

SIX MONTH PROGRESS REPORT

After visiting the Pediatrician at six months, Annie was informed that Joy was more than moderately Down Syndrome and she was definitely spastic as well. Annie was told that Joy would forever be a crib baby. Since these children seemed to be very susceptible to illness, it was deemed a real plus that she had remained healthy up to this time. The doctor informed Annie that colds, pneumonia, and other complications were often present in these babies, and the fact that she had remained well for six months was a good sign. Annie took his words as an omen that her daughter would be healed, sometime in the near future. He knew she wanted Joy healed, but admonished her not to count on Joy continuing in the good health she was now experiencing. He told her it would not last.

She was not a fussy baby; she cried at times when she hurt, but that was not often. She didn't cry when she was hungry, nor did she cry when she was wet. It became apparent to Annie these tasks needed to be taken care of on a time scheduled basis. There would be no waiting until she cried to change her, or feed her, as she had done with her two boys, who both had healthy lungs and would let you know when they needed attention.

It was only when the doctor would give Baby Joy a shot that she cried. The shot hurt; it just took a long time for the pain to register with Baby Joy. It was quite obvious Joy's message center was not operating at full capacity. Annie learned this was a common thing with many Down Syndrome babies. The doctor jokingly told Annie that Baby Joy was scaring away his patients. After the shot, Annie would get her dressed, back in the stroller and out in the reception room. While making the next appointment Baby Joy would begin to scream and cry. It took that long for the shot to finally register.

Much prayer and extensive searching began for healing, physical healing, healing like Jesus performed when he walked the earth. Every way possible open to Annie was going to be explored. In the years ahead, one day Joy would be free to run and play, laugh and talk and be all that her mother wanted for her.

About the time she reached seven months, the doctor examining Baby Joy noted that her head seemed to be increasing in size, too fast for her body and age. He called it Hydrocephalus, or water on the brain. That is both the technical term he used and one that Annie understood. He informed Annie they would keep a watch on the measurements over the next few months. Annie went directly to the library to read as much as she could find out about Hydrocephalus and also try to understand. Her findings were not very encouraging. She read about the Spitz-Holter shunt. Spitz refers to the American Neurosurgeon Eugene B. Spitz who designed the shunt. Holter refers to the designer of the valve for the shunt. This valve drains off the fluid from the brain. John Holter was unable to save his son Casey from Hydrocephalus, but his design of the valve had helped others around the world since the 1950's. Someone else who cared about his child had wanted the same thing Annie wanted, healing.

Baby Joy had to be moved from the bassinet to the crib, because she was getting too long for the bassinet. The sides of the crib were covered with padded bumpers. Sometimes Joy would get against the side of the crib and just keep bumping her head for no apparent reason. The bumpers were made and installed so she would not injure herself. She had begun to recognize, not only Annie, but her brothers as well. But when the boys went for a few days on a camping trip with their father, Annie realized there was a different reaction when they returned. It was not until they were back, being with Joy each day, singing to her over the crib, or talking to her, that she once again had recognition in her eyes. Annie was delighted to see this improvement.

7

THE MOVE TO SAN DIEGO

Shortly after this Annie learned about a clinic to be held in La Mesa, California, a suburb of San Diego. This was a week long clinic of testing and diagnostic work on Down Syndrome and retarded children. Annie made the decision to move back to San Diego. There had been considerable research in finding new ways to improve the lives of Down Syndrome children, and Annie was for that, all the way. Some of these children had learned to crawl and even to walk. Annie so wanted to take Joy there. Her sons' father gave Annie the money to rent a truck so they could make the move to San Diego.

Annie was really frustrated with this still being a man's world in the 60's. The man at U-Haul Rentals did not want to rent the twenty-four (24) foot truck to her, because she was a woman. When she had first checked into it she tried another way, rather than fight the system. She advertised on the bulletin board at Mare Island for a service man to drive it south for her. She would then pay his air fare back to the Bay Area. She waited ten days but she got no response from her ad. So back to the U-Haul Rental place she went. Annie asked to read the rental agreement for the truck. As it made no reference to gender as a requirement, only that she be a licensed driver over twenty one, she insisted that the truck be rented to her. You know, of course, this was long before equality for women. It seemed to Annie it was long before women had much say so either. She wanted to tell the man at the U-Haul truck center that being a man didn't make them responsible. She knew that responsibility was not gender based.

She did agree to pay him for an hour of his time to ride with her on the back roads of the valley in order to ease his mind. She had the ability, and also agreed to telephone him when she reached her destination with the truck. Now, having driven more than one U-haul truck over the years, she would just laugh at a guy who would attempt to keep her from renting any U-haul. She would tell him to wake up, after all! "Where was the man when you needed him?" She recognized her bitterness was close to the surface..

She rented the large U-haul truck, packed and loaded up their belongings for the trip south. The day came, the truck was loaded. Riding with Annie were Paul and the family dog, Cricket. They were finally ready to go.

Baby Joy rode with her brother, Bryan, who was driving Annie's car. He was only fifteen and a half. While he had his learners permit, he was not allowed to drive without a licensed driver in the car with him. Mother's close friend, Marie, had an eighteen year old daughter, Katie, who was licensed. She became the passenger

Annie laid down some driving rules for the trip. She insisted that Bryan drive far enough ahead of her to be out of sight. She needed to concentrate on her own driving of the big 24 foot U-haul. She trusted Bryan's maturity and did not want to be constantly checking on his driving. She insisted under no circumstances were they to leave the planned route unless they were together. They were to stop every two hours in a safe place to make sure she was still following, and had not had any problems. At each stop they made, Annie would also check on Baby Joy.

Joy was placed in her car bed in the back seat of the car Bryan was driving, with everything she would need for the trip. Katie rigged up a receiving blanket at the window to keep the light out of Joy's eyes, and she slept most of the day, except when she was changed and fed. Katie did a good job taking care of Joy while Bryan drove. It was a real adventure. Annie knew that Bryan was a good, conscientious driver. She also knew that he could be counted on for maturity beyond his years.

Cricket, the dog, and Paul were brave to ride with Annie at the helm of the U-haul. It would have been a plus to have had cell phones at that time, but this was long before cell phones. Annie had courage but was not brave enough to tackle the Grapevine Grade outside of Los Angeles. She decided they would take highway 101 to Southern California, closer to the coast. It was farther, but had fewer high hills to contend with. She was not as scared to drive up the hills as she was going down the steep grades on the southern side. She was one brave lady just the same.

Annie had made arrangements to store their furniture in a friend's garage in San Diego. She had packed the truck so that only what would be needed at arrival could be set aside. They would be living with Annie's brother, Jake, and his family until she could find a house and a job.

Well I got ahead of the story here. The first night out they got as far as Santa Maria. Annie had only to grate the gears a couple of times before she got the hang of clutching, and the whole family was ready to stop and rest. She rented a room with two double beds at a roadside motel. Katie had one bed; Mother and Baby Joy the other, while the boys, Bryan and Paul rolled out their sleeping bags on the carpet.

8

JOY'S FIRST SICK DAY

Joy had been really fussy the last hour of driving and Katie held her, giving her water to drink, but she felt awfully warm. Annie too, thought Joy felt warmer than usual and took her temperature soon after they got into the motel. She undressed Baby Joy and bathed her in cool water. As she was dressing her, powdering her warm body, she noticed the rash. On further investigation she noticed she had rash not only on her chest, but on her buttocks, and on her lower and upper back as well. Annie noticed the baby's temperature was rising a short time later, and became alarmed. She went to the office of the motel. The owners helped her locate a doctor who would see Joy late this afternoon. Annie sent Katie, Bryan and Paul to get something to eat at the restaurant next to the motel, and she drove Joy to the doctor's office.

The doctor diagnosed Joy with Roseola, or as mother later learned, baby measles. Mother told the doctor they were on the road, moving to San Diego by truck and car the next day. He advised Annie to give Joy plenty of water, and to keep the light off her the next day as they traveled. He gave her something for the fever also. Baby Joy fussed most of the night and was fully covered with rash by morning. Annie and Katie built a tent over her car bed to keep out the light, and stopped often during the day to check on her well-being. She slept most of the day, fussing some when she woke. Katie had a bottle of warm water waiting each time Joy awoke.

Without much sleep and dealing for the first time with a sick baby, they got on the road later than planned the next morning. By 4:30 P.M. they arrived in San Diego. It was the beginning of commuter traffic. Annie was getting ready to pull onto Highway 8 east in Mission Valley. They had made plans to drive the truck directly to Kelly's home in East San Diego. Since Brian was familiar with San Diego, having lived there from 1961 to 1963, Annie gave him instructions at the last stop just below Camp Pendleton. He was to go directly to Kelly's house, let Jake know they had arrived, and wait for her there.

It seems Annie had another problem. As she was making the merge on to the highway from the on ramp, she killed the motor on the U-haul truck. Directly behind her was a little dark green sport car, which looked like an MG. The driver was so close, Annie was having difficulty seeing the car in her mirrors. But she could hear him as he laid on the horn and gestured out of the window for her to "move it.". Annie was tired. Annie was annoyed at his impatience. She put the brakes on in the U-haul. She opened the door, stepped down beside the truck and walked back to the angry driver. He was shaking his hands at her in frustration and disgust.

Annie tells about walking up to the driver of this little hunter green convertible and saying, "I am a woman driver. This is my very first time to drive a U-haul truck. I have come over five hundred miles in the past two days. I know this truck rolls backward a short distance when you start it, before you can put it into gear and go forward. I suggest for your safety and my nerves you back up beside the car behind you and pray."

Without waiting for a reply, she turned, walked back and climbed into the cab of the truck. She turned the key, pushed in the clutch, and sure enough the truck began to roll backward. She stepped on the gas, let out the clutch and was able to get it to move forward. She was now on highway 8 headed east looking for the 40th Street off ramp. The man behind her did what she suggested – backed up as far as he could to give her room. She never knew whether he prayed or not, as she suggested, but when he passed her he gave her a thumbs-up out his window.

So eventually they arrived at Kelly's. They unloaded the truck later that evening after Jake, Annie's brother, got off work. Then he and Bryan turned in the U-haul truck. They drove Katie to the airport, booked a flight for her back to San Francisco, and returned after she boarded the plane and it took off.

The little family moved into Jake's small home where they would live for the time being. Jake had two children much smaller than Bryan and Paul. Joy slept in a long drawer that had been removed from the linen cupboard in the hallway. It was placed beside the couch where Annie slept. Bryan and Paul rolled out their sleeping bags and slept on the floor. Annie intended for them to be sleeping in their own beds in a very short time.

9

ONE THING OR ANOTHER IT SEEMS

Within a month Annie had the boys registered and attending school, had found a job as a waitress, and moved into a small home in east San Diego. The second night in the house all the beds had been set up. They started putting things away. For the first time in over a month, the boys would be able to sleep in their own beds. Annie was tired. She set the alarm for Joy's 2:00 a.m. feeding and went to bed herself. The alarm rang. Annie got up and turned on the light in the living room.

Annie was met with the walls crawling with cockroaches. She had never seen so many in one place in her entire life. She did not sleep the rest of the night, nor did she turn off the lights. Roaches come out in the dark. She not only checked Baby Joy's crib, but her own bed also. Then Annie went into the boys' room and turned on their lights but did not see bugs in there. She put a lamp on by Bryan's bed, and tip toed quietly out so as not to wake the boys.

The next morning, unable to reach her landlord, she called the Health Department. Annie's mother, Gertrude, and her step-father, George had moved to Alpine from Paradise two months earlier. They had come over yesterday to help, and after hearing about the cockroach infestation, were back again this morning. The Health Department inspector came. After his inspection he insisted that the landlord have the house completely fumigated. The inspector, along with Annie's step-father, George, discovered a make shift gate made of trellis material, outside over a crawl space. The crawl space was littered with dirty rags, an old comforter and garbage. The inspector insisted that the area be cleaned out before the fumigation, as it looked as if a family of dogs had slept there.

The inspector advised Annie to move out immediately because of Joy's breathing problems, and remain out of the house until three days after the fumigation was completed. He gave her a brochure on washing all the eating utensils, and anything that the baby might come into contact with. They left the house and went to stay with Jake and his family again until the place was fumigated, aired out and cleaned up. George, Annie's step-father followed up with the health inspector. They checked out the once littered crawl space before the fumigation, and advised her when they were allowed to move back in.

He and Bryan did a lot of cleaning up around the outside of the house. They hauled brush and trash to the dump. Annie was reluctant to move back into the house but had nowhere else to go. The Health Department said it was all right. They did explain to Annie again about washing every dish, pan, stainless ware in the house or anything that the baby or the rest of the family would touch before it was used. Annie and her mother, Gertrude, washed down the bathroom, kitchen, and all the window sills. They washed all the dishes, pots and pans for a second time that month, as they had done it after everything came out of storage. Annie had taken the crib with them to Jake's so that was safe. Annie often checked the beds, hers, the boys, as well as the crib, and never ever turned off the light in the room where Baby Joy slept in her crib. A blanket was always put on the carpet if Joy was on the floor, and she was watched carefully.

10

BABY JOY GOES THROUGH THE CLINIC

Joy was almost ten months old when they finally went to the clinic. Joy could not sit up, lift her head, or get up on her knees. She neither smiled nor cooed. She still slept a lot, and was eating most of her food through special nipples for gruel type, of food. Annie's brother, Jake went with her to the clinic. There Jake stayed with Annie and Baby Joy the entire time, holding Joy when Annie's arms were tired. He pushed Joy most of the time in her stroller. The stroller was elongated so Joy could lie flat. Jake transported both Annie and Joy back and forth to the hospital in La Mesa where tests were performed. These tests were done on her brain function, and she endured endless lab tests as well.

The days were spent with other parents of Down Syndrome children in the lobby- type sitting room, waiting for the next test or consultation.

Some of these children were walking, some of them talking, though not too well, and two of them, like Baby Joy, were in strollers, unable to sit up, their bodies listless. One couple, back for a second time for an updated check out, told Annie their daughter could not walk two years ago. But through patterning she was now walking. This was evidenced by her walking around and around the room rather awkwardly, but walking just the same. This child, Gloria, was having the time of her life. When she wasn't walking, she spent her time crawling through big plastic tunnels which were there for the children. A boy who looked to be about four or five crawled with Gloria. Another girl about the same age sat quietly in the corner with her doll in her arms, oblivious to the rest of us, silent, but lovingly holding her doll.

Annie so wanted Joy to be able to crawl, to be able to walk, to be able to talk. She wanted Joy to be able to laugh, to coo, to be able to go more that four hours without eating. Annie planned for a miracle. So did Jake, and they both prayed that they would get just that, a miracle. The parents of five year old Gloria had seen their daughter go from crawling to walking in a year, with patterning, a technique used to awaken damaged or dormant brain cells. Maybe Joy would one day walk, too.

The consultation time arrived. The doctor said the fluid on the brain was minimal and would not require surgery. It would need to be checked from time to time. The staff had suggested we try two things to see if Joy could progress in her physical growth. They did not offer much encouragement for her progress because of the degree of retardation, and her weak heart. They informed Annie that it was possible Baby Joy's nervous system would not be able to handle psychomotor patterning. First they explained to Annie how they had discovered that babies who learned to crawl progressed faster than those babies who just up and walked. They had seen babies with mental retardation and brain damage on a regime of patterning which developed awakening brain cells. Patterning was fully explained to Annie and her brother, Jake.

The second thing they suggested was a slide about two and a half feet high on one end, slanting down to the floor, and about eight feet long. It was to be made out of wood and finished so no splinters would result. Baby Joy was to be placed at the top of the slide three to four times a day on her stomach with her head in the direction of the lowest part. We were instructed to paste bright colored pictures along the sides of the slide. This proved unworkable, as Baby Joy would always manage to turn sideways and roll down the slide. Then she cried and fussed after each of these rolling trips down.

They decided to give the patterning a try next. They would need five people on the team. They would need to be dedicated people who would come at six thirty each morning for a few minutes, and again at six thirty in the evening, every day of the week. It was important that it be consistent in order to create brain paths. One of the team was to move Joy's head, with one on each side to move her arms and legs in a crawling, swimming motion. This was to be done in a set pattern and to a count starting with five minutes and increasing every three days. It had worked quite well with people who suffered brain damage from accidents. It increased the motor skills of some Down Syndrome children. This sounded like the treatment that Gloria, the Down Syndrome girl they met in the waiting room, had been given. Her parents had talked about something called patterning that helped their child. Annie still held high hopes for Baby Joy.

11

PSYCHOMOTOR PATTERNING STARTED

Annie was able to put together a good team. The team consisted of three people from the neighborhood, Joy's older brother, Bryan, and Annie. They were caring people and dedicated to helping Joy. Annie explained the patterning to them. (Two of her neighbors had been on a team previously for a brain damaged child hurt in a golf cart roll over.) Annie kept records on the time and noted any changes in Joy's reaction to the patterning. She could see no changes but she didn't expect it would begin to show soon. The staff at the clinic had indicated not to expect much change for some time.

The team finally got into a good rhythm on the procedure and all was going really well. They were progressing quite well from five minute sessions twice a day for the first week and beginning to build up to ten minutes, when Joy suffered her first seizure. Patterning was stopped immediately. They had been at the patterning sessions a little over two weeks now. The team stopped the patterning procedure immediately and was advised to wait for another week to ten days before starting over at stage one.

They followed these instructions, but Joy suffered her second seizure before the end of even one week's patterning sessions. The team was disbanded. Joy's nervous system could not handle patterning. Baby Joy's nervous system had been compromised. The doctors had indicated this might happen.

A little over an hour later as Annie was preparing to take Joy Elizabeth to the sitter, she suffered another seizure. Annie took Joy to the doctor instead of going to work that morning, and it was decided that a pattern for seizures had been definitely set up. Annie was told she could expect that Joy would have other seizures over time. She was given instructions on what to do, and medication as well, for Baby Joy.

Joy had now reached the age of fifteen months. She could still not hold up her head, get on her knees, and showed no indication that she would be able to crawl. She was able to roll over and she did this over and over again, until she would be stopped by some obstacle on the floor, or a wall. Then she would bump the wall or obstacle repeatedly with her head, if you did not stop her. Bumpers were put on the sides of the crib so she would not or could not injure herself. When she was on a blanket on the floor they just had to watch her if she started to roll over.

Then one day Joy was lying on Annie's bed, dressed and ready to go with Annie and her brothers for the day. Annie had bathed and dressed Joy and was getting ready herself to go to Alpine to visit with the grandparents. Bryan and Paul were beside the bed keeping an eye on Joy and bouncing the bed gently, when she actually laughed out loud! It was the first time Joy had ever laughed out loud since she was born. They bounced the bed again, but this time it turned to sadness when Joy suffered a seizure. The boys felt very bad. So did Annie. It was even more apparent that Joy Elizabeth's nervous system was stressed. After much thought, it was decided to no longer pursue any physical programs to help Baby Joy. Annie was emotionally down, physically tired, and feeling like she had run into a wall herself in search of a healing for Joy.

12

HEALING SERVICES ON THE AGENDA

Annie began taking baby Joy to healing services whenever and wherever she could find them. She was still searching and praying for a miracle. She remembered the words in the Bible that said, "Where three or more are gathered together in my name, I am there also." She believed in prayer. She attended Sunday services, and special healing services advertised in the daily paper for the week nights.

Not only had Baby Joy developed a seizure pattern, she seemed to be catching more colds, running fevers and having convulsions when the fevers shot up high. Trips to her doctor and to the hospital were beginning to escalate. Annie had not given up longing to see Joy healed. She held on to the verse in the Bible in Jesus' words to his disciples, that said, "All that I do, you can do and more." Jesus healed the sick, he restored sight to the blind, brought Lazarus back from the dead, and told the crippled man to take up his bed and walk. Surely it was possible for healing to take place today even as it did in Jesus' time.

Annie had to work and it was necessary for Joy to be cared for by a sitter part of the time. She found a wonderful lady near where they lived to baby sit Joy while the boys were in school. She was licensed to care for Down Syndrome children. She cared for another Down Syndrome girl, Gay, who came each day after attending special classes. Gay was ten years old. She also cared for Joy, who was considered a crib baby. She used the breathing apparatus on Joy at least once a day, to help her.

During Annie's second shift at her waitress job, Joy's brother Bryan, who was now seventeen, took care of Joy. Paul helped too. Bryan was able to give Joy her seizure medicine, feed, diaper and care for her. He was able to use the syringe to remove the phlegm from her throat when she was having breathing problems. He also could use the breathing apparatus when necessary to ease her breathing. Both of the boys did a good job, and were responsible and mature beyond their years.

On Sunday, Annie's day off, the boys had a day to do whatever it was they wanted. Bryan often spent the day with friends from high school, while Paul would get his fishing gear together and Annie would take him for a day of fishing at Lake Murray. He always seemed to have such a good time going fishing, and so did Bryan, visiting with his friends from high school.

One night when Annie came home from work she found Baby Joy asleep on the couch on her stomach. She was covered with one of her small light blankets. On the middle of her back was a small book. Annie looked at Paul who was sitting beside Joy watching television. She hung up her sweater and started to question him regarding the book. Paul put his hands up to his lips to hush Annie. Paul told her Joy thought that book was his hand. He said he patted her and patted her until she fell asleep, but every time he stopped she would wake. So while he slowed down the patting he placed a small book on her back. She did not wake up this time and had been asleep for over an hour. Paul figured she believed he still had his hand on her back. Paul's brother, Bryan was sitting at the kitchen table doing his homework for school.

Joy's brothers were very inventive. Joy was unable to hold her bottle, so they rigged up a holder made out of hangers, and covered it with some of Joy's old receiving blankets. All Baby Joy had to do was turn her head and the nipple was right there in front of her. Because of her breathing problems, they still had to keep a close eye on her even while she sucked her food from a bottle.

Joy's crib was in Bryan's bedroom. He was a light sleeper, and would wake if she cried. Annie came home from her second job as a cocktail waitress at 2:30 in the morning. At that time Annie would lift Joy out of the crib, change her, feed her, and take Joy to bed with her. Baby Joy would sleep there until the alarm went off and Annie got up to start another day. The boys would have breakfast and leave for school. Joy would be bathed, fed and packed up ready to go to the sitter, and for Annie to leave for work. This went on for months and months, now almost two years. Joy had not progressed at all. In fact, some version of this had been going on since Baby Joy was born.

13

JOY'S THIRD YEAR OF LIFE

Joy had now passed her second birthday. She had spent a lot more time in the hospital this past year, with very high fevers, which often caused her to have convulsions. She was often dipped in alcohol baths to bring down her temperature. Annie spent as much time as she could at the hospital. Bryan would often come and sit with Joy so Annie could go home for short periods. Jake, Annie's brother would do the same. Also Grandma Gertrude was always available to take her turn being a nurse at Joy's bedside. It was during this time, reading and asking questions, that Annie discovered how many Down Syndrome babies have incomplete nervous systems.

Before Annie had moved from the Bay Area, one day she met a Navy medic through friends. He was stationed aboard a sub based in San Diego. It was in Mare Island Navy Shipyards for repairs. He inquired of mutual friends in the Bay area where Annie and the family had moved. He called and came to visit often to see how Baby Joy was doing. He told Annie he had worked with these children in Bethesda, Maryland, early on in his career as a medic. He helped her find out as much information as possible about Joy's condition and care.

During Easter break of Joy's third year, Bryan and Paul went to spend time with their father in the Bay area. Bryan wanted to go live with his father for the remainder of his high school years, and Annie was not in a position to deny him that. Bryan had been a big help, had carried more than his share of responsibility for a soon to be seventeen year old. By living with his father, he could work, go to school and have at least a little bit of teen life. Annie realized she would have to make some different arrangements, with Bryan gone. It still frightened Paul when Baby Joy had seizures.

It was during this time that Joy's doctor informed Annie that more and more care was going to be needed. He was a very kind man. Joy was in and out of the oxygen tent, during her stays in the hospital, and those trips were getting more and more frequent. He suggested Annie make an appointment to visit the hospital for the handicapped in Costa Mesa. Annie did not like the suggestion at all, even though she was tired most of the time, and bordering on exhaustion herself. She realized there had to be a change soon.

Annie talked with Doc Andy, the medic aboard the submarine, stationed at the present time, out of San Diego. He offered to go with her to the hospital, to see whether or not she would decide to place Baby Joy there. Doc, as Annie called him, said that it couldn't hurt, and it was obvious that things were not going to improve. Annie finally agreed to go. Annie had Doc's help filling out the endless pages that were required, should Annie decide to place Baby Joy there as a patient.

The day came when Annie and Doc chose to go to Fairview. Annie could do nothing but envision Baby Joy in each of the cribs there. They were given a tour of the grounds and the hospital at Fairview. They spent considerable time in the area where Baby Joy would stay if she were admitted. Many beds were filled with babies, some younger, and some considerably older than Joy. The hospital had several floors. On the floor where Joy would be, there were six crib-like beds in each ward. Annie's heart ached as she saw these little ones with nothing but mobiles turning above their beds. Volunteers from a near-by college came during the day, and held those babies that could be out of oxygen tents. They rocked some of them in rocking chairs, holding them close and singing to them. Some of the volunteers helped with the babies' feedings. It was so sad, as none of the babies could do anything for themselves. Annie was so emotionally distraught; she had to be sedated before they left to return home. Her heart was breaking. She just could not see herself placing Joy in Fairview.

The pediatrician who had cared for Baby Joy told Annie on her next visit that Joy's heart was giving out. He said Joy needed to have her tonsils taken out to help her breathe, because they were so enlarged. Because of her heart condition, he said no one was willing to risk the surgery. He said Joy's heart was working too hard, and likened it to an old woman running around and around the block, getting more tired each time, and unable to stop and rest.

Annie still did not want to hear anymore about Fairview, and put it out of her mind for the time being. Annie was tired too; she stopped working the second job so she could stay home with Paul and Joy in the evenings. Paul missed his brother immensely, as they were good company for each other. He needed some tender loving care also. Annie discovered Paul had been marking the days off on the calendar until summer. Then he would spend summer with his brother at his father's, in the Bay area. The boys had spent every school vacation and the summers with their father since the divorce. Paul had earned that time, and it would be good for him too, to be out from under the pressure of having to help care for Baby Joy. When the time came for Paul to leave for the Bay Area, Annie told him that if he wanted to stay for the next school year, she would allow him to go.

Paul had been afraid to ask her if he could go live with his father, but Annie sensed how much he missed Bryan. Things would be easier for him up there. Paul was going into the tenth grade. He could work on his father's projects and go to school and have a lot more freedom than she could offer him here. Annie's heart was heavy but she knew she had to let him go. She said goodbye to him at the beginning of summer, and he left to go live with his father, a step-mother, and his brother. After he had gone that day, Annie cried for a very long time.

It was a sad month after Paul left. She would come home from the sitter's, to the house, with Baby Joy and it would be so dark and quiet. There would be no one to talk to about the school day. There would be no cup of hot coffee made, sitting ready for her to drink on the dining table. There would be no quickly washed dishes on the drain board that Paul had finished just before she came home. She had no one with whom to share the happenings of her day, only silence, and more silence.

Annie realized she was going to have to make some changes. She no longer had need for a two bedroom unit where they had lived this past year or so. Even the small lawn they had been taking care of at the front of their unit was too much for her to do.

Not long after Paul had left for the Bay area to be with his father, there had been an attempted break-in at Annie's unit. She called her neighbor, a Navy man who lived next door with his family. He had been there for Paul and was good to both of them, and would have done anything Annie asked, to help with Baby Joy. He came over immediately and searched the entire area but found no one.

Annie had been sitting at the desk in the dining area when she heard the door knob turn. Whoever had tried to break in before, was trying again. Annie remained totally quiet with only the desk lamp on. She felt great fear. About a week later, Annie's unit was broken into during a time when she was at work. The neighbor on the other side of her unit saw a man leaving by the kitchen door. She called the police and told them. They were unable to find anyone to apprehend.

Annie had nothing of value to steal. Even the television had quit working. However, she did discover later that birth certificates, car papers and insurance policies were missing. They had been in a small safe about the size of a shoe box in the bottom of a closet. The box had been jimmied. These papers were of no value to anyone else. The papers were returned to Annie over a year after she had moved out of the apartment complex. The landlord had found them in a storage unit after renters had left. It took the landlord some time, but he was finally able to locate Annie and return the papers to her. The landlord believed that the renters who had that storage unit were guilty of the break-ins, reported in the neighborhood.

14

DOWN SIZING

Annie moved from the unit in the six apartment complex to a small one bedroom apartment over an old closed antique store in the heart of North Park. She still worked as a waitress as it was always easy to get another employee to take her shift if Joy was ill or in the hospital. If she had been working in an office, her job would have been in jeopardy, taking that much time off. Grandma Gertrude came and stayed with Joy while Annie worked the lunch shift. The lady who had cared for Joy for almost two years now took her during the evening shift on nights Annie worked.

Annie was off work by nine almost every night. She stopped by and picked up Baby Joy and returned to her apartment. The apartment was quiet and clean, as it had been the living quarters for the lady who, prior to her death had operated the antique store. It had a private driveway so

Annie's car was off the street. The store and apartment were in back of a much larger two story home. There was only room for a bed and dresser in the bedroom, so the crib became part of the living room furniture. Many nights Annie sat at her desk and wrote on the typewriter, playing music on the radio to break the silence. Annie was close to Joy here and could monitor her breathing, and take care of her needs,

She had located another healing service to take Joy to on Wednesday evening. Wednesday was her early day off work so she would be home by six at the latest. Annie prayed that somehow this would be the answer, that God would heal Baby Joy. That was the only thing Annie wanted now. Her two sons were happy with their father; he was good to them, and could do for them in ways she was unable to at the present time. Annie was dedicated to devoting her every minute away from work, to finding a way to heal Baby Joy. Annie was still spending all of her spare time reading about healing for Joy.

15

JOY IS AN ORCHID

On one of those evenings at home, Annie sat reading about healing in the Bible, and writing on her typewriter. She had closed her eyes for a moment and her question to God was, "What am I supposed to do?" She prayed with her head down on her crossed arms on the typewriter, and cried softly. Suddenly in her head she heard the words, "Joy is an Orchid." She listened. She heard the words again, and still she waited, listening for more words.

Annie raised her head, rolled a clean sheet of paper into the typewriter, and typed across the top, "**Joy Is An Orchid.**" She listened. Then she heard the next line. She typed that, and then the next, until a two page poem had unfolded on the paper in front of her. Annie knew she had not written the poem. She had heard it word for word. It was June 16, 1968, it was about 11:30 p.m., and she was alone in the apartment with

Baby Joy. She had never experienced this type of inspiration before. She looked at the words. Annie knew in her heart of hearts that it was the answer she had asked for. She also recognized that it was not the answer she had been praying for, because she wanted Joy healed. This poem was about acceptance, about uniqueness, and about care. The poem is included here as part of Baby Joy's story.

JOY IS AN ORCHID

God gave to me an orchid plant potted and lavishly tied; He informed me of her specialness but I thought I was so wise.

My garden is filled with roses of every shade and hue; So I planted my orchid amidst them where she could be loved and viewed.

I knew what my roses needed to be watered and sprayed and fed; So I gave the same care to my orchid but she didn't unfold in this bed.

Though I called in the best of experts their advice was sadly disclosed; For I wanted to keep my orchid in the same bed as the rose.

I pleaded with all of the gardeners to help me in my plight; They looked at my withering orchid shook their heads and left in the night.

They wanted to tell me my orchid belonged in her little green home; but they loved me, I guess, so they left me, to find this out on my own.

One day as I looked into her upturned face her eyes bespoke her cry; "Show her, dear God, how to care for me, I am your gift, please show her why."

God answered her plea, revealed to me a rose needs an outside bed.; An orchid's an orchid, a flower 'tis true But a hothouse plant instead.

Then I lifted up my weak little orchid and down the pathway I fled; replanting her limp little body in her very own special made bed.

Now, as I work among my roses while I tidy up their beds; I smell their heavenly fragrance and touch their soft velvet heads.

Then down thru the lathe topped walkway to the greenhouse I am led; To see unfoldment more each day as I leave her there in her bed.

I loved my very special orchid, she too, was a gift from God; She's doing better in the greenhouse and she greets me with a nod.

I keep her there in the greenhouse and give her love and special care; And today she took a blue ribbon at God's own Orchid Fair.

I learned a very wonderful lesson from my Orchid and my Roses too; They both reflect God's allness but more, God's Oneness, too.

Annie got the gist of the poem. She felt it was telling her that Joy needed to be in a place where she would get twenty-four hour care, but Annie still wanted to give healing a chance. The following two Saturdays, Annie rode the bus to Los Angeles to attend healing services. They were being conducted in a large auditorium by a Kathryn Kuhlman. Annie held baby Joy in her arms for the entire trip. When the bus parked, the driver got out Baby Joy's special elongated stroller.

Annie noticed people arriving in ambulances, wheel chairs, and her heart was filled with hope for Baby Joy. There were hundreds of people at both of the services, some went forward when Kathryn Kuhlman called them from the audience and prayed for them. She laid hands on their foreheads, and some were overcome with the spirit and fell to the floor. Some were singing with joy when they got up, for they had been healed. No one seemed to be able to just walk up there for healing without being called. Annie prayed and prayed Kathryn Kuhlman would point to Joy, who Annie still held in her arms.

Both trips were big disappointments. Both times Annie cried silently most of the way back to San Diego by bus. Her arms were aching from holding Baby Joy the entire round trip. Her heart was heavy and her spirits were at a heart breaking low ebb.

The San Diego Tribune had an advertisement that caught Annie's eye. It said that miracles were taking place at this church on Wednesday nights. Annie needed a miracle. Annie was praying for a big miracle.

She was not sure miracles could be classified as big or small. A miracle was a miracle and she prayed for one for Baby Joy.

Wednesday evening she parked her car, got out the stroller, and wrapped Baby Joy warmly in a blanket. She pushed her across the street and into the church. The service had not yet begun and Annie wheeled the stroller down to an empty row on the side. Here she parked the stroller beside her as she sat in the aisle seat. Annie wanted to be close enough to carry Joy forward for healing when that part of the service was reached. There was no one sitting in her row. In fact there were only a few people sitting in the center section of the church so far, but more were starting to come in.

Shortly a man about six feet tall, bald headed, dressed casually and neatly, came down the side aisle and into her row. He sat down beside Annie. She noticed that a cross hung on a chain around his neck and rested on the front of his shirt. At first Annie felt annoyance. With all the seats still empty, why was he sitting beside her? The prelude music began in front of the church, played by a lady at the pipe organ. More people began to come into the church and take seats.

Then he introduced himself to Annie as John, and asked, "May I hold Baby Joy?" He had called Baby Joy by her name. He said he would carry her forward for healing at the end of the message.

At first Annie hesitated, but felt like this was an omen, so she handed baby Joy and her blanket to him. He was so tall that he could lay Baby

Joy on his lap with her legs up his chest, and her head held firmly between his hands on his knees. He folded up the small blanket and put it under her head. He never took his eyes off Baby Joy's eyes. He looked at her like he was reading a book. He was softly speaking to her. Annie was unable to hear the words because of the music playing. Baby Joy seemed to recognize him. Joy had stopped fussing almost immediately. She seemed to be looking right back at him. It reminded Annie of someone who had been waiting for a friend to come down the lane, and finally spotted the friend in the distance.

The music came to an end and the congregation joined in some singing. Then the preacher took to the podium to deliver his message on healing. He spoke the same words Annie had railed at God about. "What I do, you can do, and more," Jesus had said to his disciples.

The time came to call for those who desired healing to come forward. John stood holding Joy in his arms even as Annie stood ready to go forward with her daughter. He carried Joy forward and three of the clergy laid hands on Joy's head and prayed. Nothing happened. Annie was once again in despair. She was not sure God's word meant anything. She was filled with doubt about her faith in God. Joy was still the same.

Annie turned to take Joy from John's arms but he said he would carry Joy to the car for her. Annie was in tears, as she pushed the empty stroller and followed John with Baby Joy, out to the car. He placed Joy in her car bed, covered her, buckled the strap across the middle and secured the baby. Then he took the stroller, folded it and put it in the car behind the front seat. Through her tears Annie thanked him, and bid him good night.

John turned to Annie and said, "Call her Margarite. You two shared a lifetime in France. She was a street urchin and you befriended her. You took her in, you loved her, you educated her, and she loved you. She knew when she came back this time, you would accept her, and care for her. Call her Margarite. She has memory of that name."

With that John said good night, crossed the street and walked away into the darkness. Annie never saw this man again. Annie never heard of this man before or after. Annie had done some reading on reincarnation and past lives. She had read articles and a book on past life experiences, but all of this was too much to take in. Joy's condition and this information only added to Annie's confusion about what to do for her.

Some months later during one of Joy's hospital stays, she was running an extremely high fever and something happened that caused Annie to remember John. She had come to the hospital in a police car, as Joy was having convulsions. Annie dared not strap Joy into her car bed. The policeman drove them to the emergency room. Then the policeman took Joy from her arms and ran ahead into the hospital to get help. He made sure Joy was taken care of.

Then he turned to Annie and told her if she needed a ride home or someone to bring her car to the hospital, he would see that it was done after he was off duty. The policeman handed her a card with his phone number on it. He was so kind and Annie was grateful.

Joy was in and out of alcohol dip baths that night. Her fever finally came down. Annie never left her side. The next night after work she relieved her mother, Gertrude, so she could go home. Annie was nodding off in the chair by the crib when a nurse came in to check on Joy and to talk with Annie. She insisted that Annie take some time off and get out of the room. She suggested Annie go across the street for something to eat. She assured Annie the nursing staff would keep an eye on Joy.

Annie went outside. The night air was cool, and it felt good to breathe the fresh air. Annie didn't realize how tired she was. She felt like she could sleep for a month non stop, and knew she was keeping awake by shear will. She had something light to eat, and drank a couple cups of very strong coffee. Then carrying another coffee to fortify her for the next few hours, Annie walked back across the street to the hospital.

When she entered Joy's room she felt a presence, and noticed a plain silver cross pinned to the blanket hanging over the head of the crib. It had not been there before Annie went to eat. Annie wondered where the cross had come from, and questioned the nurse at the nurses' station about visitors. The nurse informed Annie no one had been in the room since she left, except for the nurses. None of the nurses knew anything about how the cross became pinned to the blanket hanging on the head of her crib.

Much later that night, or was it early in the morning, Annie wasn't sure, but she remembered where she had seen that cross before. The man named John, who had told her to call Joy, "Margarite," was wearing one just like it the evening he had held the baby, the evening he sat down beside her during healing services in the church on Park Avenue. Why had no one seen him come into Joy's room tonight? Why had he not left a note? Why had he not waited to talk with Annie? Annie was filled with questions, but dozed off a short time later in the chair in Joy's room. The cross remained on Joy's bed until she took her home, although Annie never found out how it got there.

When Annie unpacked Joy's things after reaching home with the baby, she discovered a booklet in the bottom of the bag that held her things. The book had a shocking pink cover, and silver letters. It was entitled, **"LOVED."** There was no author listed. It was a book that had been put together by someone who had typed it. Annie read the book. She became more aware of how her wanting Joy to be healed was bordering on selfishness. Annie was not ready to acknowledge this outwardly just yet, but she realized she had been vaccinated with the idea just the same. The idea that wanting Joy healed was not what Joy wanted, began to creep into her thoughts little by little, day by day.

16

HEALING IS RELEASE

A Short time later, Annie made an appointment to go speak with the Unity Minister at his San Diego church. Grandma Gertrude was one of the charter members of this church. It was here at this church that Annie first discovered a God of Love. This was over six years ago now. Annie has since read every book she could get her hands on, about this God of love, and about healing. Since then, she's needed her own answers, not answers from others..

It was warm out the day she went to the rectory. Joy was dressed in a little blue and white polka dot dress, anklets and a pair of white baby sandals. Joy was in her stroller because she was now over 36" long. Baby Joy was dead weight to carry for any distance or to hold in Annie's arms for even a short time. She pushed Joy to the rectory door, where she was greeted with a warm welcome by Rev. Stevens.

Annie talked to him about healing. She shared with him the many healing services she had attended in San Diego and San Diego County. She shared with him about her two trips to Los Angeles by bus to Kathryn Kuhlman's healing services, as well as the long rides back in despair. She shared with him her disappointment. Annie shared with him some of the excuses she had been given for instant healing not taking place. She did not share with him the poem she had heard and written down. She did not tell him, either, about the man John who had told her of a previous lifetime with Joy.

Annie wanted to know why her prayers were not being answered. She wanted to know why Joy was not being healed. She wanted to know what Jesus meant when he said, "What I do, you can do and more?" She was questioning if this God stuff was true at all.

Rev. Stevens listened. When he spoke, he said he could understand her longing for Joy's healing. He could feel her love for Joy, and he agreed all of those words were true. "But sometimes, Annie, we don't want to hear God's answer. Instead we want it our way." Then he asked her, "Have you ever considered that release could be healing? Release Joy to be all that she can be, and then let that be what Joy wants, not what you want. Annie, you need to accept Joy just as she is. She came for a reason you cannot see. Annie, you need to let go, and let God."

Instantly, Annie's anger surfaced. Instantly she was filled with frustration and stood up and answered sharply, "Sounds like another cop-out to me, by another minister of God." With that Annie spun the stroller around, went to the door and opened it before Rev. Stevens could even get to his feet. She went out, slammed the door not too gently, and left. She burst into tears and cried all the way to the car. She continued to cry while she put Joy back into her car bed. She put the stroller in the back seat and drove away. Annie was filled with anger. Her heart was breaking.

That thought of selfishness was pushing its way back into her thoughts again. She was not being selfish, she contended. She loved Baby Joy. Was it wrong to want her to be able to live life fully?

Annie felt she had now received another disappointing answer to add to the many excuses she had been given by ministers who preached from the pulpit on healing. This was about the sixth rectory Annie had visited after a healing sermon, and had challenged the minister to back up his word.

"Release, that is all I ever have to do," she exclaimed to no one but herself. "Release her sons' father from their marriage because he wanted to play the field and not be married any longer. Release Jeff, Baby Joy's father because he didn't want to acknowledge his daughter, or to be in her life either. Annie had to release her sons, too, to go live with their father for the few teen years they had left. Now was God going to demand she release Joy too? Was release placing Baby Joy in the hospital in Costa Mesa? Was release what the poem she heard told her to do?"

Annie just could not consider the ramifications of what release would mean at this time. It was another idea that was going to haunt her many moments of thought and prayers for weeks to come. Annie's thoughts started to skirt around what release meant.

It was probably six weeks later, one night, when she read a story about walking in another's shoes. Annie was thinking what it would be like to walk in Joy's shoes. Was Annie wanting for Joy something Joy didn't want for herself? She was drawn back again to the silver cross still hanging on Joy's crib, back to the booklet she had discovered in Joy's bag some time before. This was the book that first got her attention about being selfish, and wanting it her way. Was she going to have to give up someone else she loved? Annie was thinking about this after she had finished the story she was reading. The idea wouldn't leave her.

How long, she wondered, could she go on before she ran out of ministers to challenge about healing? Did she want Joy to be healed for any reason other than what Joy would want? Joy couldn't speak, and Annie had spent hours trying to put herself in Joy's situation, in Joy's body, and asking that nagging question that would not go away, "If I were Joy, would I want out of this body?"

Weeks of tossing this idea of release back and forth followed. The idea reverberated in her mind until Annie felt weighed down with grief and sadness.

17

YOU ARE TRYING TO HEAL THE WRONG PERSON

One night Annie came home from work and after feeding Baby Joy and putting her down for the next four or five hours, she sat down at her typewriter to write. Instead, she wound up on a crying jag. She cried until there were no more tears left. She remained with her head down on her arms in silence, totally at a loss for an answer. It was dark outside. The only light that shone in the room came from a night light in the kitchen behind her. The windows were open to allow the breeze of early fall to cool the living room. There was no sound outside except the call of a cricket in the shrubbery below her stairs. Just silence. Just silence, Joy's breathing and Annie's exhaustion were present.

"You are trying to heal the wrong person," the voice said. It was a gentle, soft-spoken voice. It seemed to come from across the living room.

It was a voice filled with caring, a voice filled with warmth. Annie could feel the love in this voice, and in the words. It was a voice she had never heard before.

She looked up from her desk; she looked over at Baby Joy who was asleep in the crib. Only the sound of breathing filled the air. There was no one in the room. The only over stuffed chair was empty. The sofa was empty. No one was sitting in her living room.

Annie had heard this voice; she had audibly heard the voice. It was not the silent voice she had heard once before when the words to the poem about "**Joy Is An Orchid**" came to her. This was an audible voice. This voice was definitely audible; it touched her heart, like nothing had ever done up to that moment. She knew she had heard the words. Then she repeated the words she heard to herself. You are trying to heal the wrong person. Who else was there to heal in this room but Baby Joy, she questioned?

Annie waited for more words. She searched the room with her eyes to make sure no one was there. Only Annie and Baby Joy were in the room. Annie was even more certain she had heard the words audibly spoken by a male voice.

Suddenly she realized what the words meant. It was as if someone had taken the lid off a jar and let the words fly out in her face with force. Annie jumped to her feet. She was wide awake. She was alert. She turned to where the voice had come from and with force answered, "I am not retarded! I can take care of myself! I don't need to be healed, Joy does! Do you hear me, I am not retarded!" She repeated these words several times and then collapsed on the sofa in tears and cried until every part of her body ached with grief. Finally, Annie fell asleep.

The alarm woke her at 2:00 a.m. She was still on the sofa. She was still dressed in pajamas, robe and slippers, the way she dressed every night after she came home from work. Annie was acutely aware of what had taken place prior to her falling asleep. She was more certain each time she thought about it, that she had heard the words audibly, because of the tenderness and love in the voice that had spoken.

She fed Baby Joy, changed her, and put the breathing mask on her for a short time, before laying her back in her crib to sleep. Annie was exhausted. She crawled into bed. Exhaustion took over. She soon fell asleep. It was a troubled sleep, full of dreams that seemed to go nowhere but back to where they started. Annie had dreams of Joy crawling on the bed, of trying to climb up on the bookcase headboard of Annie's bed, and Annie reaching to bring her back down. Annie had dreams of Joy crawling to the edge of the bed, and Annie catching her before she fell off. They were not the dreams of the crib baby that Joy was. Annie woke and went to the crib to see if Joy had been healed, but her same baby daughter, Joy Elizabeth, that she so loved, lay there asleep.

Morning arrived. She was remembering her dreams. She fixed some coffee, bathed and dressed Joy, and waited for Grandma Gertrude to arrive. Annie wanted to tell her mother about the voice, and yet at the same time she didn't want to tell her. Annie didn't quite know why she was so uncertain about telling her mother what she had heard. Maybe she was concerned that her mother would think she was losing her mind. It had crossed Annie's mind as well when she got up this morning.

Annie's mother arrived early that morning to stay with Joy so Annie could go off to work. While Annie fixed her mother a cup of coffee she decided to share with her the experience of last night, the total hopelessness she was feeling, the crying until she couldn't cry any more. She shared with her about the voice she heard. Annie shared with her about the dreams, in the early morning hours, of Joy crawling all over her bed. When she finished relating the experience, her mother told her to sit down. Then Annie's mother shared something with Annie that she had never told her before.

Her mother said, "When you were a little girl, you never spoke an audible word until after you were four years old. No amount of coaxing, no amount of cajoling by either me or your father could get you to speak out loud, to talk. Your father and his parents were sure you were dumb, and they blamed my family for your condition, because I had two nieces who were both deaf and dumb. Your father often called you dummy, and we quarreled about this on many occasions.

One day his parents had been to the homestead for the day and had commented on how sad it was that you were dumb, and what a shame it put on the family. We had a really bad argument.

It was then I insisted that you be taken to the nearest big city to be examined. Your grandparents were involved in the argument and looked at me as if I had lost my mind and could not see what was what. They were taking sides. I would not give up until your father and his parents agreed with me. Your father was reluctant at first, but I stood my ground, and we made an appointment to take you to the city to see a doctor who specialized in children.

She went on to say, "Annie you were not like Joy, however. You could walk, you could play, you crawled at seven months, walked a little past your first birthday. You just didn't talk! You would stand or sit by the hour when you were alone and stare off into space. I often felt you were seeing a totally different world than the one we were living in at the time. You never talked to your doll as your sister Ellie did to hers. In fact, Annie you rarely ever played with your doll. You just seemed to be satisfied to sit quietly and stare off into space."

Mother went on telling Annie, "We took you to the city and the doctor did some tests, examined you, and then made time to talk with us about you, much later that week. He met with us. After the testing had been done and the results were in, his words were like a cool drink on a very hot day to me. He was a very wise doctor, a very wise man."

"There is nothing wrong with this child," he said, "She doesn't talk because she doesn't have anything to say. But God help you when she does, because you are going to wish she had an 'OFF' switch."

Mother continued, "Your father wasn't sure the doctor knew what he was talking about, but I felt great relief and I told him right there in the doctor's office that I never wanted to hear him call you dummy again, or to discuss it with his parents. To me the doctor's conclusion was right and perfect."

With that mother stood up and gave Annie a big hug. She looked at Annie and told her, "I should have shared this with you a long time ago. I never thought you were dumb in the first place, and I put up with the accusations and names for way too long, but the doctor was so right.

"When we left the farm and moved to the city, you had already begun to talk. Once you started school, you often talked so fast that your father would repeatedly ask you to slow down or turn it off. Often times your answer to him was, "I have to talk so fast because I have so much to say."

That morning as Annie left for work, a peace filled her heart; a quiet calmness had permeated her being. She felt like she had been wrapped in a cocoon of love, of gentleness. The feeling remained with her the entire morning. Her lunch shift at work went by fast and she returned mid-afternoon to the apartment, to Baby Joy, and her own mother sitting in the chair reading.

Annie realized she wasn't filled with anxiety as she had been these past weeks. She wasn't trying to push down anger all of the time, and remorse for not having found a way to heal Baby Joy. She was wrapped in the feeling of peace and calmness, a feeling she had not experienced for a very, very long time. She thought often during the day about the dreams she had that morning of Joy crawling all over the bed and trying to climb up on the headboard. She wondered if she was seeing a Joy free of that body that did not seem to work. Was she seeing the real Joy?

That night after she finished the dinner shift, picked up Baby Joy at the sitter's and returned home to her apartment, the peace was still there. Joy's breathing seemed less labored than before. She ate almost a full jar of baby food before she took her bottle.

Peanut butter on the spoon handle pressed against the roof of her mouth seemed less a hassle before feeding her. The food from her first few spoonfuls seemed easier for her to swallow. Oftentimes putting the peanut butter on the roof of her mouth, so she could remember how to swallow, seemed such a challenge for Annie and Joy. Tonight things flowed. Soon she was asleep in her crib, the lights were turned off, and Annie fell into bed herself and into a deep quiet sleep.

The weekend was here. Annie had been thinking about the words she heard, about what her own mother had shared with her about her early years. Until much later she could not remember those days before she started school. Annie remembered her father telling her many times to slow down when she talked. Annie remembered many other times when he told her to "turn it off."

She read again that poem that she had heard and written on the typewriter, and decided to share it with her mother the next time she came to baby sit. Annie thought about what Rev. Stevens had said about release being healing, and she looked at her baby and said, **"I want what you want, Joy. I want what God wants for you, not what I want."**

Annie was at last ready to let go and let God. She was finally ready to release Baby Joy to what Joy wanted and needed. She wanted that peace that had been with her since the day she heard the words, **"You are trying to heal the wrong person."** Annie could not remember when she felt such peace ever before. She could only describe it as a feeling like being surrounded in a cocoon of warmth and love. She wanted that for Joy, too.

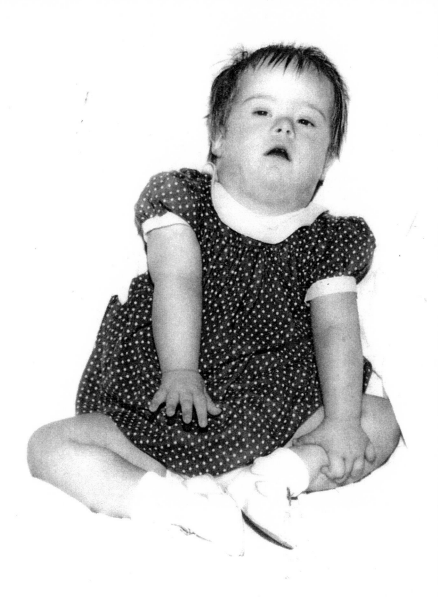

This picture was taken of Joy Elizabeth in September, 1968.
Joy was into the third year of her life.

I am ever grateful to the photographer for his patience and
love as he has baby Joy on his lap on a pillow, and with
one hand holding her head up and taking the picture with
his other hand.

18

TO FAIRVIEW HOSPITAL

Within the next week, Joy took a turn for the worse, and was hospitalized in an oxygen tent for almost five days. When she came home, Annie, with her brother Jake, drove Joy Elizabeth to Fairview Hospital in Costa Mesa, where she could get twenty-four hour care. It was a hard decision for Annie. She had to leave Joy and not see or visit her for ten days. This was a requirement of the hospital to allow Joy to become acclimated to the ward and to the nurses who would be caring for her. She was in a room with five other terminally ill babies, some in much worse condition physically than Joy, but all needing constant care. This was the ward for twenty-four hour crib babies.

When Annie returned home, her sister-in-law had removed the crib, the changing table, and the stroller from the apartment. She had also packed up all of Joy's things, boxed them and placed them in the storage room downstairs. She wanted to make Annie's trauma of coming back to the empty apartment and the empty crib, less shocking. It was going to be hard enough for Annie to come home without Baby Joy.

This had to be a labor of love for the sister-in-law because she was pregnant at the time. She had often sat and held Joy and prayed for her and helped with her care. Ironically, nine months later, Annie would be doing the same thing for her sister-in-law and brother, when their new baby, David died of SIDS in his bassinet shortly after being put down to sleep. While Jake and Sharon made preparations for his funeral, Annie packed up their nursery, boxed up his baby things, and placed them along with Joy's in storage. Annie now remembered how she cried almost the entire time she was doing it, mourning not only their loss of David, but of Joy as well, even though Joy was still alive at Fairview.

Annie drove to Costa Mesa every weekend after Joy's ten days of acclimation. She spent Saturdays at her bedside, holding her hand inside the oxygen tent. Joy was allowed out of the tent to be fed her bottle and Annie would sit in one of the rocking chairs in the room to feed her. Annie stayed at a place near there, and attended church on the grounds on Sunday.

One Sunday Annie had an eye opening experience at the church and healing service held at Fairview. She always wondered just what was going to take place as she sat and watched those patients at Fairview come into the service. Some of them walked in, some of them were very spastic, some came in wheel chairs pushed by volunteers, but they all seemed so happy. She wondered if this was where healing was going to take place?

That Sunday, the singing and sermon had ended and the pastor from a local Baptist Church called for healing. One tall young man, very spastic, was making his way forward for healing. When he reached the pastor he held out his hand revealing a bandage around one of his fingers. He asked for prayer to heal the finger he had caught in a car door the past week.

Annie sat in total awe. Here was a young man so spastic he could hardly keep his balance as he walked down the center of the church for healing, wanting healing for a smashed finger. He evidently had found total acceptance for the condition that had him living here at Fairview, but his smashed finger he wanted healed. Annie left the church service with a new look, a new feeling, a new sense of acceptance.

On Sunday afternoons she joined a group of other parents, some single mothers, some couples, and one father who always came alone, for counseling in the community room of the hospital.

He was a fireman and father of the baby next to Joy. His daughter had been there for over two years. Her name was Gayle. She could make sounds, and was much more spastic than Joy, but helpless, every bit as helpless as Joy was. The fireman said the baby's mother had never come to see her, but he was there once during the week and every Sunday.

This was their only child. Annie shared with him that Joy's father had left, never acknowledging the baby. Once, the fireman walked over and tapped Annie gently on the shoulder. Annie had been leaning half way onto the foot of Joy's bed and had fallen asleep. He said he was afraid Annie was going to fall.

After the counseling sessions, Annie spent about a half an hour longer with Joy, and then set out in her VW Bug to drive back to San Diego. This was how Annie spent her weekends from the middle of October, 1968 until February, 1969.

Annie recalls one time when she was coming back to San Diego from Costa Mesa in a heavy rain storm. She had left later than she had planned and had been crying while she was driving. It was beginning to get dark. Suddenly, the windshield wipers on the VW quit working. She had to pull into the median strip because she could not see out of her windshield. She sat there with her head on the wheel, crying. It seemed to Annie about all she did was cry. Her emotions always seemed so raw after the counseling sessions at the hospital on Sundays. It was hard too to leave Baby Joy and return home to an empty apartment alone.

Annie hadn't noticed the patrol car pull into the median strip behind her until she heard a rap on her window. She looked up and lowered the window. A Highway Patrol Officer stood by the car. He could tell Annie had been crying. He inquired if she needed help. She told him the wipers had quit, and she was headed back to San Diego from Costa

Mesa, where her daughter was hospitalized. He checked a couple of things, and then told her to lock her door and he would return shortly. He pulled back on to the freeway and she saw his blinker lights through the rain, indicating he had turned off at the next off ramp.

In about twenty minutes the patrol car pulled back behind her VW. The officer got out and came up to the car. As he approached, Annie rolled down the window. It was still raining hard. He took out his knife and also a large potato which he cut in half lengthwise. He then proceeded to wipe the cut side of the potato on the windshield for a few seconds. Then he handed both halves of the potato to her with these words, "This will keep the windshield clear enough to drive about fifteen or twenty miles. Then you will need to rub the cut side of the potato across the windshield again. You will probably have to do that three or four times before you get home, but you will be able to see."

Annie looked at him dumbfounded. He went on to tell her his father, had been a truck driver who always carried a potato with him. He would be driving the truck uphill, steering with one hand and leaning out and wiping the driver's side of the windshield with a raw potato. This was before they had hydraulic pumps to run wipers.

Annie thanked him, put the potato on the seat beside her, and pulled back onto the freeway towards home. The officer followed her for a short distance before turning off. Annie did have to stop once again at Del Mar, and once in north San Diego, before she reached her apartment in

North Park. She kept that potato even after she had the wipers fixed. She kept it in her glove compartment until it was dried up and black. She felt so grateful to the patrolman who stopped that Sunday night and helped her.

At the time she never considered how God sent just the right officer to her aid, one who knew how to clear a windshield when the wipers failed. It was only later, much later, when Annie began to think about how things worked, how everything unfolded when she got herself out of the way and let God work. This experience and the earlier experience, at church had begun to happen more often, even though at the time Annie was still feeling her loss too much to appreciate them completely.

19

THE NEW JOB

After Joy was hospitalized, Annie promised her mother she would quit being a waitress and get a daytime job that was not so hard. Annie was able to get a job, very quickly, as a dispatcher for a two-way radio communications service company near where she lived. Soon Annie would be able to begin putting more money into the medical and hospital bills she owed.

Soon Annie would find a smaller, less expensive place to rent. A friend at church had told her about a place in Spring Valley, a very small old house that was going to be available soon. It would be half what she was paying in San Diego proper. It would mean a longer drive to work. Her friend promised to look into it for her and to keep her posted on when it would be available.

Annie knew she could live frugally and pay down on the medical bills she had piled up above what medical insurance paid. She had stayed in that waitress job for another reason beside it being easier to take time off when Joy was ill. The union had medical insurance, and while that medical insurance paid a lot of baby Joy's bills, it didn't come near to paying them all. She was very deeply in debt. She had no medical insurance with the new job, so she had to stay well herself.

Annie liked her new job. She enjoyed the dispatching. Annie's employer knew about her hospitalized daughter, and was aware that if and when the time came, she would need time off. He had agreed to that. He was aware of where she went on the weekends, and let her keep to herself on Monday's when she returned to work, quiet, sad and withdrawn. He never questioned her sadness, only asking on one or two occasions if there was anything he could do to help.

One of the engineers found her, in the tube room taking inventory and crying softly. Apparently he had been told about her daughter Joy, so rather than probe, he just asked if he could help in anyway? When she shook her head, he left, closing the door softly behind him.

Annie settled into her job without any problems. She had worked in offices before, once for eleven years with the same company in the bay area. She was used to doing many jobs that a small business such as this required. Her new job with the service company kept her busy. The multi-tasking fit right in with the dispatching of technicians. This was a rather busy service center for two-way radios and pagers. The company not only serviced equipment, but two installers were scheduled daily to put new equipment into police cars, fire trucks, construction vehicles, and remove old equipment from out-dated vehicles.

Annie was charged with keeping the Technician's FCC licenses up to date. She did this by keeping up-to-date records of their customers' installed equipment, maintenance and services as required. She was well organized and did a lot of the maintenance scheduling that the FCC required. Annie dispatched technicians to jobs, as well as sending them out on emergency equipment calls.

There were three outside technicians, two installers, her boss and Annie in this service center. Their chief job was to keep the Motorola equipment they carried, in tip top condition. Each of the technicians maintained many customers. One of the technician's maintained over two hundred pagers and a paging system for the Doctors Service Center in San Diego. They all helped locate lost and stolen pagers, and once even restored a pager that had been rescued. It had dropped in the bay from a boat at dock side. It was interesting work. Time between weekends with Joy sped fast. It required scheduling regular maintenance on the Repeater sights as well, both in San Diego and on Otay Mountain southeast of Chula Vista.

One of the Engineers, Gil, asked Annie to attend the small party the company was having with their parent company in Oceanside. Annie was to be part of a foursome, the boss, his wife, and Gil. This was the first time she had been out sociably for several years. There was fun, a good dinner, and awards that were presented to some of the men. It was nice to be included. Annie was not much into the party spirit, but she liked the people she worked with. Annie's mother said it was good for her to go.

Annie had spent the weekend at Fairview after the company party on Friday. She went back again early on Monday morning to Fairview, as Joy had developed pneumonia and was having difficulty breathing. Annie came back to San Diego that night, and returned to work on Tuesday morning. It seemed like weeks since she had attended the company award party, and little was said to her or from her about it. Annie did remember to thank her boss, telling him she appreciated that he and his wife had included her in the party.

20

THE SWEETWATER SHANTY

One day Annie's friend at church told her the little house in Spring Valley was for rent. She told Annie it wasn't fancy but the landlady lived next door and wanted to rent it. It was less than half what Annie was paying here in San Diego, so she rented the house the very next week.

It wasn't much. That was an understatement! She immediately called it her "Sweetwater Shanty" because it left a lot to be desired in comparison to her neat little upstairs apartment. She decided she would make it work. It was so old it had gas pipes in the ceilings where gas lights used to be suspended. It had two bedrooms, both exceptionally small, and not a closet in either one; in fact the only closet in the place was a few narrow shelves built into the hallway between one of the bedrooms and bathroom.

The bathroom seemed to have been an after thought, as the ceiling was a foot lower than the bedroom. One tiny window, about the size of a sheet of paper, was all the outside light it had. There were no towel bars or rings in the bathroom, not even a hook to hang a towel on so, Annie guessed the former tenants just threw towels on the floor. It had a very small shower, but no bathtub.

Annie decided first off to get one of those spring loaded towel poles, and found one at a near-by thrift shop. She put it up. As Annie pushed the spring load section into place, it went right through the ceiling of the bathroom. Well, this was going to be a challenge, she decided, making the house work for her. She bought a lid from the paint store at the small strip mall about a block away. She painted it the color of the ceiling with a bottle of craft paint she purchased, and it became the cap for her towel bar. At least the problem of where to hang the towels had been handled.

Not having any closets in either bedroom called for more creativity. She could not afford to buy an expensive or even a second hand wardrobe cupboard at this time. So Annie, with her mother's help, decided to build one in the second bedroom. There was a recess in that room where, probably at one time, a wardrobe cabinet had stood. Annie and her mother framed in a closet, put a piece of plywood on top for a shelf, and hung a clothes pole underneath it. They installed a curtain rod across the front and hung plastic curtains on it to keep the clothes clean. Annie did not have a lot of clothes, as she had been wearing uniforms for work for at least five years. She barely had enough to fill the closet space. She put light weight boxes on the shelf above. This bedroom was very small and Annie didn't have anything to put into it except her clothes, a chest of drawers and a small table lamp for light, which she placed on top of the dresser. She hung a plastic window curtain to match the one on the closet she'd built.

The other bedroom, off the bathroom on one end was only big enough for Annie's double bed and a floor lamp. There was no overhead light in that room. In fact there were no ceiling lights in either bedroom, or in the living room.

The kitchen did not have any built in cabinets, either above or below, only an old fashioned stand. This was the sum total of kitchen storage. The stand had three drawers, a flour bin, and two doors above the work space which was about three feet wide, and twenty inches deep. There was an apartment sized stove in the kitchen, a metal service cart and a shelf along the wall. The kitchen was so small Annie's refrigerator had to be put in the dining room.

The dining room was the largest room in the house. It was a very different room, with bookcases along the fifteen foot wall. There were three shelves built in the bookcase.

The back door opened into this room. Annie put her desk in here because there were plugs and an overhead light. Annie's small dinette table and chairs made up all the furniture in the room.. Her refrigerator lodged on the wall closest to the kitchen. She used the book cases not only for books in one section, but dishes, pots and pans, and the few appliances she still owned. She kept her folded sweaters in one part of the bookcase too.

The only window in the room was beside the back door. It overlooked a large thorny cactus plant just outside the door. That cactus snagged one of her sweaters once on the way in at night and unraveled a good piece of the sweater before she discovered she was tethered to it.

Across from the back door outside, were her driveway and a so called carport. She would park her VW in there for the time being. Even the carport was old and leaned a bit. Later in the winter, Annie chose not to park in the carport for fear it would collapse on her car during rain and wind storms. She made the right decision about that, as it did collapse during just such a storm come winter time.

The living room was the worst room in the house. It was wall papered with garish, loud, unattractive wallpaper. It made the walls feel like they wanted to reach out and grab you and send you reeling backward. Annie still had the recliner which would no longer stay upright unless it was propped against a wall, a two piece corner sectional, a square corner table and one end table. She still had her three bulb hanging, oriental lamp stand. This now had to be reduced to two because one of the globes had broken in a move. Since the lamp had been custom made, it was beyond her pocket book to replace the globe.

Annie asked the landlady if she could strip the wallpaper from the walls and paint the living and dining rooms. The landlady was delighted about her wanting to fix it up, and not only bought the paint, but did not charge her any rent for the first two months of Annie's stay. It was either remove the wallpaper and paint or not go into that room at all. The wallpaper had been overpowering.

Annie visited Baby Joy on the weekends, and spent her week nights, after coming home from the office, peeling layers of wallpaper off the walls. Once she opened the front door after much tugging. There were weeds at least waist high just beyond the two foot by three foot front porch. She closed the door; locked it and never opened it again while she lived there.

It took Annie almost a month to remove the wallpaper and in so doing she uncovered two double wall plugs that had been wallpapered. She was not sure they were safe to use. Annie could only work so long on wallpaper removal, as the dust got into her throat and she would wind up coughing for more than an hour, and couldn't go to sleep. One day during lunch break at work, she mentioned about uncovering the two plugs that had been wallpapered. She asked one of the communications engineers how to tell if they were good, as she didn't want to have a fire. Gil, who had invited her to the Company party, offered to stop by on his way home from work and check them for Annie. He did, and they were good, so the next morning he brought two plug plates to work and gave them to Annie. She was delighted about the plugs because she had been using an extension cord running from the living room into the dining room. Now she had workable plugs in each room.

Finally, Annie got all the wallpaper off. The walls were ready to paint. Her brother, Jake, in the mean time had found some cabinets someone was throwing out. He brought them over and helped Annie install two of them in the kitchen.

Then Annie started on the painting. It was already close to the holidays, and Annie hoped she would have the place looking a little more like home at Christmas. She painted two of the walls, and then decided before she painted any farther she would do the ceiling in the living room. There was no ceiling fixture, only the stubbed out gas pipe, so it should be a quick job. Annie covered her furniture with plastic sheets. The next night she came home from work ready to complete the ceiling which was not very large. The room probably was no more than twelve foot by twelve foot. She painted almost the entire ceiling, working her way towards the corner where the doorway to the dining room and the bedroom met a hall. She had turned off the wall furnace earlier, and it was beginning to get cool in the room. Annie filled the roller pan for the last time with paint, put the can of paint below the ladder so she would not step in it when she got down, and climbed the ladder to finish up the ceiling. After only about four or five swathes with the roller, the roller went through the ceiling.

This part of the ceiling was made of butcher paper! Soot, black soot, came down everywhere. It was in her hair, on her face, in the roller pan of paint, even in the can of paint under the ladder. It was as if she had opened an old unused coal shoot. She really had a mess now, and she looked like a mess as well. She got down off the ladder and burst into tears. What more could go wrong, she thought.

Annie called the landlady who immediately came over with her husband. They both looked rather sheepish, as they explained to Annie what had happened. It seems there had once been an oil heater in the place. When it was removed the ceiling had not been properly replaced where the flue pipe had gone up through the ceiling. The landlady assured Annie she would have it repaired the next day, and they would replace the ruined paint.

Annie cleaned up the mess, and herself. Leaving the furniture covered, she went off to bed. Annie was disappointed that the painting was going to be delayed and the ceiling unfinished. She was exhausted from frustration, more than she was tired. It would be at least three days before she could start to finish the painting in the living room.

A week later Annie had the living room painting finished. She had painted the dining room, as well as the small hallway. It looked clean and uncluttered and very very nice. The landlady brought over a room sized rug to put on the living room floor. It made the room seem much cozier. The wood floors underneath the rug and in the dining room were well worn, and probably had never been waxed. They needed to be refinished but that was beyond Annie's ability. The two uncovered plugs now working, plated and in use, and most of her stuff looked nice. The plastic sheets had been stripped off the furniture; finally it was beginning to have some semblance of home for Annie.

Annie hung the only wreath she had, on the back door, strung a few garlands of red and green tinsel on top of the bookcases and set out her two Christmas candles. That would have to do for Christmas. She couldn't afford to send out cards, and besides she was not too into the spirit of the holidays. But she was grateful she had a place to live and could put more of her salary on the medical bills she still owed. She would have to start paying rent next month, as she had already been in the little Sweetwater Shanty over two months now.

21

TO DRINK OR NOT TO DRINK?

Annie had to make a second emergency trip to Fairview during the first week of January after Joy suffered a set back, and the doctor had given Joy adrenalin. Annie was off work for two days. Joy rallied and Annie came home after a long talk with the doctor in charge of the baby's care. He advised her to make arrangements for Joy's funeral so that when the time came it would be much less of an emotional trauma. He advised her Joy's heart was giving out.

Annie had never heard of such a thing, and she came home again crying almost the entire way. How could you make plans to bury someone before they even died? Annie had driven home in the steady falling rain again on a dreary and a very sad day for her. Not only was it raining outside but she was an emotional bucket of tears herself. Annie should have called the minister, but she didn't. She should have called her brother, Jake who was always there for her, but she didn't. She came home and wandered around in her little Sweetwater Shanty of a house for the next two hours. She found herself going aimlessly from room to room like a fly afraid to land because it might get swatted. She hadn't eaten anything since breakfast, but she was too beside herself to think of food.

Finally Annie got into her car and drove down to the small strip mall shopping area, about a block and a half away. Here she parked her car, locked it and went into the little neighborhood bar. Annie knew the bartender; she had met both him and his wife before. She knew he worked at the bar, and knew his wife was the lady at the checkout stand at the little grocery store next door to the bar. Mike, the bartender, was a nephew of Annie's landlady and they lived about two doors south from his Aunt in a fairly new home.

Annie told the bartender she wanted to sit at the end of the bar and drink; she did not want to be disturbed. She did not want to talk with anyone. She did not even want to think tonight. She gave Mike the keys to her car and told him to send her home in a cab if he thought she was too drunk to drive. Annie told him she would come down and settle up tomorrow. Tonight she just wanted to drink until she couldn't think any more.

Mike realized she must have received bad news about her daughter. Mike and his wife, Ginny, were both aware of Joy's situation. One time the three of them had coffee and a gab session with Annie's landlady's next door. Mike and Ginny were in and out of their aunt's place often, as she was more like a mother to Mike than an aunt. The landlady was on Annie's call list from Fairview Hospital too.

The bartender, Mike, took her keys and set her up a drink. She sat there drinking slowly, trying not to think about what the doctor had suggested. She ordered another and then another. After that, Annie doesn't remember much. Mike, good to his word did not give Annie her keys to drive home. He called his wife and she drove Annie home after she got off from her job at the store. She took Annie's keys, opened the door to the dining room, and made sure Annie was inside. She locked the door, leaving the keys on the dining room table with Annie's purse.

Annie stumbled into the bedroom, but before she could get undressed she became violently ill, and fled to the bathroom where she was deathly sick. She awoke in the wee hours of the morning, cold, lying on the bathroom floor, with a head as big as a watermelon and aching everywhere her body could feel. Annie managed to get herself to the bedroom. She slept the rest of the night in her clothes, rolled up in the quilt on top of the bed.

The next day was a work day. Annie had to go to work. She had already been off two days. Her head ached, her mouth felt like she had eaten a bucket of feathers. Even a shower did not make her feel any more human. She changed her clothes, walked down to get her car, and drove into San Diego to work. All day she felt lousy. All day Annie wondered how people could drink like that week after week and still function. She felt physically worse than she would ever have imagined she could feel, and while it did stop the thinking for a time, she was not sure it was worth the way she felt today.

Annie was having problems even concentrating. She was hurting, and her body felt like somebody had beaten it with a hazing paddle. She was afraid to eat anything because her stomach still felt like it wanted to rebel at her for the unusual drinking she did. Annie managed to get through the day, however. It was one terribly long day.

Before she left work, she finally made the call to the Unity minister, and set up an appointment to take care of Joy's funeral arrangements. The minister recognized her agony over the request. He tried to assure her that it was done much more often than she would have thought. He told her it was often requested by a spouse, who may have been the sick one, or a care taker, or someone close. He explained it was done so that, when the time came, emotions would not overrule the dying person's requests.

Annie realized that what she had done last night was not the way to take care of her problems. It was a form of running from them, through booze. Annie had used it to still her mind, but wound up wondering how people could choose that way to solve problems. It was much more painful than thoughts about making funeral arrangements had been.

Annie drove back down to the bar after work to pay Mike for the cab fare, and to thank him, only to find out that his wife had driven her home. Ginny came over on her break from the grocery store and the three of them shared a cup of coffee together. Annie shared with them what the doctor had said, and told them she had an appointment for the following afternoon to make the necessary arrangements. Annie felt she had lost more than a whole day yesterday, because for a part of it she was too drunk to care, and later she felt so dismal that it wasn't worth repeating that experience ever again. Mike and Ginny understood, as they had become good friends to Annie.

January passed; the weather was terrible. It rained more days this winter than it didn't rain. Finally, on one of those rare clear days, Annie did some laundry at the Laundromat in the mall. To save money, she decided to hang the wet laundry out on the clothes lines strung up in her back yard. She had used them once when she first moved in last fall.

Annie was busy hanging out her wash when the landlady came running over, waving her arms frantically and telling Annie to get out of the back yard. Annie had hung clothes out there before, and besides, this was the first day it hadn't rained for days. Her landlady admonished her to stay out of the back yard while it was so wet, because an old cesspool still remained and could cave in during such wet weather. Annie took her word for it, and those clothes she had hung out remained there for over a month, and needed laundering again before they could be worn.

Annie knew how dangerous an old cesspool could be with the ground saturated from so much rain. It continued to rain off and on the rest of January.

22

YOU ARE NOT ALONE

Every weekend Annie continued to go up to the hospital in Costa Mesa. The weather always seemed to be bad on weekends. She would park her car in the lot and run into the hospital. At the end of the day she would run back to her car and go to the place where she stayed overnight.

Joy didn't seem to get any better, but neither had she suffered any bad colds lately. The doctor said her heart was very tired, and she definitely was losing weight. Her reddish brown hair clung to her head like it had been slicked down with water. Annie always put her hand into the oxygen tent, and laid her thumb in Baby Joy's hand. She would clasp it tightly. Annie knew Joy did not recognize her, but it was comforting to feel her little fingers curled around her thumb. Baby Joy was very pale these days.

Annie found the counseling sessions on Sunday harder and harder to participate in. She rarely shared anything about how she felt, but listened to the others. They too cried often, and shared the heartache they were feeling. But on this Sunday, Annie finally broke down and shared. Annie was grieving about the day the doctor told her Joy was going to die soon. She shared her experience, deciding and making arrangements ahead of time. It was here she unburdened her night of drinking to drown her grief, and to keep from thinking, and how awful she felt the next day at work.

Annie wondered afterwards why she had held onto her grief so long before sharing it with the few parents who attended these gatherings. All of them were parents of a child on the terminal floor. All of them were facing the same situation as Annie. Though some of them would face it sooner, others had already had their son or daughter on the top floor for over a year. Joy had only been there for three and a half months.

Three nights after the session with the support group at Fairview, Annie found herself back into the role of victim in despair. She kept hashing over and over her thoughts about the unfairness of life. Annie had wailed about having to go through this pending death of Joy alone. She railed at having to be alone at Joy's birth. She cried out in anger about her feelings of Baby Joy being abandoned by her father.

She lamented about having to face by herself all the set-backs and sicknesses Joy had endured since her birth. She felt so alone. She was alone, and down in the dumps. She needed to face that. She no longer had her sons for solace, and she no longer had Baby Joy at home. Annie was into the worst victim-state-of-depression she had encountered for many months. She didn't consider, however, going to be anesthetized by drink again. She knew that only made the pit she was in seem even deeper, darker, and harder to get out of.

The more Annie sat in that recliner chair propped against the wall and thought, the more depressed she became. There didn't seem to be any light at all at the end of the tunnel, not even a star seemed to be shining in the sky of her life any more. Life went on outside her house; in here it seemed to be like wallowing in a sea of darkness and fore- boding. It had been raining most of the day. She was not only wrapped in this dark state, she felt cold, alone, and totally desolate.

She had been reading, but dropped the book on the floor and sat there brooding. She didn't bother to turn on the lights even though darkness had settled in. It seemed like the walls were coming in and crowding her into her corner.

Then out of the silence she once again heard that audible voice, that soft voice, so filled with tenderness, so gentle, yet so profound, and the words she heard were, **"You are not alone. You have never been alone. I am with you. I have always been with you."**

There was no one in the room. Annie was completely alone, but she had heard the voice. She had heard the words, and the veil of her grief and sadness lifted like a curtain going up for an ovation following a great play. It was only seconds later when Annie arose from the chair, turned on all the lights in the house, and began walking from room to room singing the Hallelujah chorus. She was not alone! God was with her! She repeated the words over and over as she continued to move about the little house. Never before had words exemplified the power that those words held for her. Never before had Annie gone from such a place of despair, to such joy as she felt at that moment, here in her little Sweetwater Shanty, the first week of February, 1969.

23

HIS WORD IS TRUE

On Friday, February 7th, 1969, Annie received a pleasant surprise. Gil, the engineer, called and asked her to go out with him. It was Gil who had invited her to be part of the foursome to attend the company party last October. He was the electronics engineer who volunteered to stop by and check the uncovered outlets in her living room. Annie knew he was separated from his wife. Her boss had shared with Annie that Gil's wife had run off and left them the day after Christmas last year. She knew he was a father with four boys at home and a daughter who had just recently married.

Annie accepted the dinner date, but took a rain check on the movie because of her early trip to Costa Mesa the next morning. Gil said he would pick her up about six thirty. Annie was nervous! She had not been on a real date for over four years, and was not even sure she knew how to act or what to wear. What would she wear, anyway, she asked herself? She wore pants suits to work.

Annie's wardrobe didn't have much in the way of dresses. Should she wear the olive green wool jersey with the matching stole? It was classy and fit well the last time she wore it, although she was thinner now. It always brought compliments when she did wear it. Then she remembered she didn't have any brown heels to go with that dress, so that was out.

The dress she wore to the company party was too dressy to wear to dinner. Besides Gil might think that was the only dress she owned. He would be pretty much right on that score.

Her wardrobe was definitely sparse. She was acting like a teenager, with nothing new to wear. Maybe Annie should just wear her black velvet pants and the long sleeve white jersey top she usually wore to church. At least she had black heels to wear. Finally she decided on that.

Annie also decided to go down and gas up her VW so it would be ready to go early in the morning. She wanted to be at the hospital in time to talk with the doctor before he left for the day. He did his weekend rounds before eleven. So off she went, down a couple of blocks, to gas up her car.

When Annie returned from the gas station there was a note on her door to come over to the landlady's house right away. She lived next door. Annie rushed over, hoping to hurry back, shower and change before going out to dinner. Mrs. Malloy answered the door. Annie entered the warm cozy kitchen where the landlady was baking cookies. They smelled wonderfully good. Annie realized how hungry she was.

She had hardly pulled her coat off when the landlady told her the hospital had called. Mrs. Malloy was on Annie's phone list from Fairview. She said the hospital had called right after she had seen Annie drive out her driveway. The hospital told her Joy had taken a turn for the worse, and Annie should come immediately.

Annie thanked her and hurried back across the path to her little shanty. She tried to call Gil and cancel the dinner plans. One of his sons's answered the phone. He told Annie his Dad had gone out for the evening. She said all right, and didn't leave a message, even though the son asked if she wanted to. While Annie waited for Gil, she packed her over-night bag, grabbed a book, and made a cup of instant coffee. She was glad she had taken the time to go down and get gas. A few minutes later, Gil drove into the driveway.

Annie hurried out to meet him at the car. She was still dressed in the same clothes she had worn to work. Annie told him she was sorry to cancel the dinner invitation. She told Gil she had tried to reach him before he made the drive over, but one of his sons said he had already left.

Gil offered to drive Annie to the hospital, but she told him it was in Orange County, in fact in Costa Mesa. He answered by telling Annie he knew how to drive to Costa Mesa. Gil asked Annie to give him five minutes to make arrangements with his mother to stay with his sons all night. Gil suggested they take her VW. Should she decide not to come home for any reason, in the morning he would take the bus back to San Diego.

Arrangements made, Annie gave Gil the car keys and tossed her overnight bag and book into the back seat. She sat in the passenger seat, clutching the cup of coffee in her hands for warmth, more than for drinking. She wished she had made a cup for Gil as well, but she never expected he would opt to drive her to Costa Mesa. Fifteen minutes had elapsed since she tried to call him at home, and they were backing out of the driveway to head north to Costa Mesa.

She cried some on the drive up. She explained to Gil about her daughter's condition, and that she was in the terminal ward at Fairview. She was silent a good share of the drive. Gil did very little talking also. Annie was alert to the off ramps and street turns they needed to take to Costa Mesa and the hospital.

They arrived before nine. Waiting for them in the downstairs sitting area were Annie's older brother, Bud and his wife, Eileen. They had not been able to reach Annie, and had decided to drive up to be with Joy. Not knowing whether Annie was on her way, or not yet home from work, or out, they decided not to let Joy be alone.

They were second on Annie's call list. Annie was thankful, and gave them both a hug. The couple was waiting down stairs to be cleared, to go up to the ward, when Annie arrived with Gil. She introduced Gil to her brother and his wife, and pushed the button to announce she was here. The four of them took the elevator to Joy's floor. Annie went immediately to be with Joy; they went to the sitting area to wait.

Joy was in the oxygen tent, as usual. A nurse and a doctor were at her side. Annie could see Baby Joy was having difficulty breathing. They had given her adrenalin earlier and she had rallied some. The doctor told her Joy had been having considerable problems breathing most of the day and it was getting worse as the evening came on.

Annie slipped her hand inside the oxygen tent. Joy wrapped her fingers around Annie's thumb again. Then Joy opened her eyes and looked at Annie. The fingers grasping her one thumb relaxed and Joy closed her eyes. Her breathing became even more labored, but she was still fighting. Annie went to talk to her brother, his wife, and Gil in the waiting area, but returned shortly to Joy's bedside.

The rest of the ward was in darkness, as the babies had been put down for the night. A nurse was going from crib to crib checking on each of them. A curtain had been drawn around Baby Joy's bed, and a soft light glowed at the head of her bed. The nurse came every few minutes and checked on Joy, then returned to her station where the doctor sat writing at another desk.

The doctor laid down what he was writing, stood, and came over asking Annie if she had taken his advice about making arrangements for Joy. Annie fished in her purse and drew out her billfold and the card the mortuary in San Diego had given her. She told the doctor she had signed the papers and brought them with her, agreeing to an autopsy at time of death. Annie felt if anything could be done that would help future babies with Down Syndrome it would be what she wanted. She had put herself in Joy's shoes once again, and knew it was what Joy would have wanted.

Annie left the ward one more time and went to the waiting room to have coffee with her family and Gil. The nurse had taken them a pot of coffee and cups, and told Annie to take a break and go have coffee with her family. She promised to come and get her immediately if there was even a small change in Joy's condition. Annie had almost come to the conclusion that the adrenalin shot had rallied Joy enough so she would probably be better by morning. She decided she was going to stay at the hospital either way. Her brother, Bud, offered to take Gil back to Annie's house in Spring Valley, for his car, so he would not have to take the bus.

Annie had hardly finished half her coffee when the nurse came hurrying in and Annie left to go to Baby Joy's bedside. The doctor was with Joy when Annie came back into the ward. Annie could see she was having a difficult time, and begged the doctor not to give her any more adrenalin. He said by law he had to do that. However, before he could prepare the shot, Joy opened her eyes one more time, closed them, and she was gone.

Annie closed her eyes too. Once again the dream she had of Joy crawling onto the headboard of the bed, and being pulled back from the edge, flashed through her mind. Was she seeing Joy's soul, free from this body that didn't work? Annie wasn't sure, but she knew in her heart of hearts that Joy was now in a much better place.

It was well past 2:00 in the morning when Annie finished with the paper work and saw Baby Joy for the last time. Annie was weak, shaking, numb and in shock from the sense of release she felt for Baby Joy. The doctor was concerned with Annie's shivering and recognized she was in shock. He offered to give her something to calm her nerves, but she refused to take any medication. She informed the doctor she was not driving, and would be all right once she was home and got warm.

The four of them left the hospital around 2:30 in the morning. Realizing that no one had eaten anything since noon yesterday, except coffee, they decided to stop at a nearby twenty-four hour restaurant to have some breakfast. Annie wasn't hungry and spent most of the time pushing the food around on her plate, managing only to eat her toast and drink some more coffee.

It was while her brother Bud and Gil were talking about their similar jobs that Annie realized she was not alone! She had not been alone tonight when Joy died. Her older brother, Bud and his wife, Eileen, were with her. So was Gil, the man from her work who had asked her out to dinner tonight.

Inside her heart she felt the joy of those words she had heard just three nights ago. Annie recalled hearing herself singing the Hallelujah chorus; the same way she experienced it the night the voice had spoken **"I am always with you. You are not alone."** She was not alone now.

It was then Annie suddenly realized she had accepted the message she had heard in her living room as real, as coming from God. The acceptance resulted in the manifestation of not being alone at the time of Joy's transition. Not only was part of her family with her, but a friend, and most of all God. She stopped pushing the food about on her plate, and began to eat, feeling hungry for the first time in a very long time. Maybe she was feeling for the first time something other than the dull ache that seemed to be like a suit of armor she had been wearing for months.

When breakfast was over, they parted company in the parking lot. Bud and Eileen got into their pick up truck and left for Claremont Mesa where they lived. Gil opened Annie's door, and after she got in, he walked around to the driver's seat to drive back to Spring Valley.

Annie was still feeling chilled. Gil said he would turn up the heat, but she said no. Gil reached into the back seat and got a large throw he had seen there and put it around her. She always kept it there, for often times Annie's mother came up with her and always felt cold. Many times Annie had taken it with her into the ward where Joy was, and put it over her own shoulders when she was sitting there by Baby Joy's bed.

It wasn't going to be dawn yet for another hour or two, and the traffic was light. The sky was clear, and they had been on the San Diego 405 freeway for some time. It was quite possible Gil was not going to get home to his boys much before time for them to get up. He had not slept at all; neither had Annie, but she attempted to keep up a conversation so he would not get too sleepy while driving.

While they were driving back, a shooting star shot across the horizon bright as bright could be, and lit up the pre-dawn sky with its brilliance. Annie took it as an omen from Joy. Maybe this was Joy streaking across the universe, letting Annie know she still lived on. Annie felt at peace. She felt like a heavy load had been lifted off her shoulders. She remembers taking some deep deep breaths and releasing some very long sighs on the ride back to Spring Valley.

When Gil parked her car in the driveway, it was after five thirty in the morning. He asked Annie if she was going to be all right alone here at her house. She told him yes, she had to make some calls this morning. She needed to let her sons know Joy had died. She needed to call her younger brother, and to let the minister who had helped her with Joy's arrangements know. There were other calls she needed to make too.

But for now all Annie wanted to do was go to bed and feel warmth clear through to her bones. She still had the chills and shakes.

Gil offered to call later in the day. Maybe she would like to go for a walk on the beach if she was up to it? She left that open. He bid her goodnight. No, good morning, he corrected himself with a smile. Annie thanked him for driving, for being with her. She watched him back out of the driveway and head for his own home where his four sons waited for him.

She later learned he arrived home to find his second son in the downstairs family room, folding the papers for his paper route. His son had asked him if he was just coming home from going out to dinner. His other three boys were still sleeping. So was his mother, who had come over from next door to stay with the boys. This was the arrangement he had made before he could drive Annie to the hospital in Costa Mesa.

24

SHE CAME TO HEAL

Joy's memorial service was held in the Unity Church of San Diego on Valentine's Day, 1969. Only the family, some of the employees where Annie worked, and her close friend Marie from the Bay Area, were present. The poem, **JOY IS AN ORCHID** was read as part of her memorial service. The Hallelujah chorus was played. Joy was free!

That night Annie's brother Jake took Annie, her two sons, and their mother and step-father George, as well as Annie's friend Marie, out to dinner. Marie had come to stay with Annie and had been there for three days now and not left the little Sweetwater Shanty except to go to the services today. Jake, Bryan and Paul took it upon themselves to show Marie San Diego at night, while Annie and the rest of the family returned home. They must have had a good time because for years it was rumored that Marie owed Jake a boat trip. By the way Marie and Jake were married eighteen years later.

It has been many years since Joy made her transition. Annie has gone on with her life, living but never forgetting the lessons she learned in wanting to heal Baby Joy. She learned about taking responsibility. She learned about what it means to release. She learned about letting go and letting God.

Annie thought for years that letting go was being out on a limb ready to fall, and sawing off the limb at the trunk. What a picture that was in her mind, and it followed that she only let go when there seemed no other way. Now she has learned that letting go is a choice, a choice she makes day by day to just be where she is. She knows she doesn't have to have everything her way. She continues to learn this lesson again and again, year after year. Annie knows Joy healed her life, and she has come to the conclusion that her life, as well as Joy's, was perfect just the way it was.

Annie realized that early on she had made a decision never to run away again. Before she was finished with this experience of wanting to heal Joy, she learned you can run from things in your mind, even more than you can run physically when things are bad. Annie has reached another level of not running now. She has had to give up wanting to fix everything and everyone in her life, and she accepts life just as it is. She is still learning and she knows now in her heart that everyone will be shaken gently or violently awake, at some time in their life experience.

Annie is learning to let things be as they are. It is a challenge to stay in the present and not want to be working on the future in her mind. It is almost as big a challenge not to step from the present into the past, where laying blame on others is a habit. Annie is learning not to be judgmental. She is learning. Slowly at times, she is realizing that she doesn't have all the answers, but is open and willing for the answers to come to her without resistance. Annie has learned a lot about forgiveness. It has become her goal to heal every relationship that she has left unhealed this time around.

Annie has continued, too, to see the wholeness that she is, the beauty that she exudes, the love that she feels for others and herself. She learns to experience joy and creativity that has reached its time, and awaits birthing. Annie has begun to sense that perhaps she is only a character being played in God's book called life. She plays the part well when she doesn't try to rewrite the script in her own image, or demand it be played her way or no way. Annie knows the choice is hers to let go and let God.

Annie believes that once in every lifetime experience, someone comes along and it seems like they come to throw a monkey wrench into living. They come into the person's life for a reason. They spiritually grab the shoulders of the intended; then continue to shake them gently into awakening. Sometimes they shake the intended vigorously to get their attention.

Joy Elizabeth was just such a person. She came to heal, not to be healed. She drastically changed the life of her mother Annie, and for almost four years of her life she shook that person called Annie awake to wholeness. I know, because, I am Annie and this is my story, mine and Baby Joy's.

She Came to Heal is the gift Joy Elizabeth came to give. Annie feels privileged to be able to help wrap this gift, and tie it with ribbons of joy. She joyfully adorns the top with a shooting star, and presents it to Joy, and from Joy, with love. May whoever reads these words know what a precious gift Joy Elizabeth was. You can be sure she has taken a blue ribbon at God's own Orchid Fair.

Addendums

Annie married Gil a year after Joy's transition. A company policy forced her to leave her job where Gil worked. She worked for eighteen years for a company in Chula Vista as Office Manager, while she helped raise Gil's four sons. They still remain in close family contact, though she and Gil parted after the boys reached adulthood and left home. She is in touch with Gil by E-mail and they share yearly visits in Arizona. Annie joined his sons', his daughter and their families in helping Gil celebrate his 80th birthday in Scottsdale, Arizona in October, 2006.

Annie's brother, Jake who along with Joy's two brothers, Bryan and Paul showed Annie's dearest friend Maria San Diego. It was Valentine's Day, 1969. Some eighteen years later, both of them single, Jake returned from his job in Saudi Arabia and went to visit with Maria in Idaho. She planned a sleigh ride, dinner in a tent and party in Sun Valley, Idaho. A few days later he proposed to her. They now live in Twin Falls, Idaho, and raise orchids for a hobby.

Printed in the United States
132603LV00004B/4/P

9 781438 910864